Introduction to Probl

A guide for :

Hoger Onderwijs Reeks

Dit boek maakt deel uit van de *Hoger Onderwijs Reeks*. Deze reeks dient ter verspreiding van onderwijskundige informatie die het gehele hoger onderwijs betreft, dus zowel het wo als het hbo. De redactie is samengesteld met dat belang voor ogen.
De redactie richt zich op drie groepen: studenten, docenten en beleids-functionarissen/bestuurders. Studenten kunnen de informatie gebruiken bij de inrichting en vormgeving van hun studie. De informatie voor docenten is vooral bedoeld als ondersteuning bij de inrichting en uitvoering van hun onderwijs en als basis voor nadere onderwijskundige professionalisering. Voor beleidsfunc-tionarissen en bestuurders levert de reeks een bijdrage aan het denken over het hoger onderwijs en draagt hij informatie aan die van belang kan zijn voor de beleidsvoorbereiding en het nemen van beleidsbeslissingen.

De reeks verschijnt onder auspiciën van de Contactgroep Research Wetenschap-pelijk Onderwijs (CRWO), het landelijke samenwerkingsverband van de univer-sitaire centra voor Onderzoek en Ontwikkeling van het hoger onderwijs.

Prof. dr. Th.J. Bastiaens (Fernuniversität Hagen/Open Universiteit Nederland)
Dr. H.J.M. van Berkel (Universiteit Maastricht)
Drs. T.J. Dousma (Stichting Surf)
Ir. M.P. van Geloven (Digitale Universiteit)
Prof. dr. J.F.M.J. van Hout (Universiteit van Amsterdam, voorzitter)
Dr. J. van Keulen (IVLOS Universiteit Utrecht)
Drs. M.I.M.A. Mathijssen-Jansen (Hogeschool van Amsterdam)
Prof. dr. P. van Petegem (Universiteit Antwerpen)
Dr. J.N. Streumer (Hogeschool Rotterdam)

Redactiesecretariaat:
Noordhoff Uitgevers
Hoger Onderwijs
Hoger Onderwijs Reeks
Postbus 58
9700 MB Groningen
www.noordhoffuitgevers.nl

Introduction to Problem-based Learning

A guide for students

Jos H.C. Moust

Peter A.J. Bouhuijs

Henk G. Schmidt

Noordhoff Uitgevers Groningen/Houten

Ontwerp omslag: G2K Designers, Groningen/Amsterdam

Eventuele op- en aanmerkingen over deze of andere uitgaven kunt u richten aan:
Noordhoff Uitgevers bv, Afdeling Hoger Onderwijs, Antwoordnummer 13, 9700 VB Groningen,
e-mail: info@noordhoff.nl

Met betrekking tot sommige teksten en/of illustratiemateriaal is het de uitgever, ondanks zorg-
vuldige inspanningen daartoe, niet gelukt eventuele rechthebbende(n) te achterhalen. Mocht u
van mening zijn (auteurs)rechten te kunnen doen gelden op teksten en/of illustratiemateriaal in
deze uitgave, dan verzoeken wij u contact op te nemen met de uitgever.

3 4 5 6 / 13 12 11 10

ISBN 978-90-01-70730-9

NUR 841

Preface

All over the world, universities and colleges are offering an increasing range of educational programmes based on the problem-based learning (PBL) approach. Problem-based learning requires students to engage in a lot of self-directed learning behaviour. This approach does not prescribe in great detail what and how students should learn. Students have to take the initiative themselves to find explanations and solve problems. Teachers facilitate and guide students in acquiring subject-matter knowledge and skills as well as helping them to become life-long self-directed learners.

Experience has shown that a good preparation for working in a problem-based learning context is important. This book is based on our long experience with problem-based learning at Maastricht University. It offers students a practical introduction to this educational approach. The book pays particular attention to the skills students need to operate within as well as outside problem-based tutorial groups. Special attention is given to methods of structuring satisfactory discussions of the various types of problems students get confronted with, as well as techniques for chairing tutorial meetings and how students can best organise their studies in a problem-based learning environment. Tips, exercises and questionnaires are designed to help readers get a better grip on their learning processes.

This second edition of *Introduction to Problem-based learning. A guide for students* is a thorough update of the first edition. We present more information about recent insights in learning and teaching and the way problem-based learning fits into these developments. More attention has also been given to the various skills students have to employ in a tutorial group. A new chapter is devoted entirely to the role of the discussion leader. Special attention is given to cultural diversity in applications of PBL in order to make this book a truly international introduction for students.

In our view this is the perfect survival guide for students in a PBL environment.

Acknowledgements

We would like to thank numerous colleagues and students at Maastricht University and other places around the world who have given us feedback while we were developing the components of this book. The illustrations were drawn long ago by Chris Voskamp for the very first local version. We would particularly like to thank Corien Gijsbers for adapting parts of an internal manual for students, and Mary Lawson and Andrew Davies who were so helpful in translating the first edition of this book.

Maastricht, April 2007
Jos Moust, Peter Bouhuijs and Henk Schmidt

Contents

1 Features of problem-based learning: An introduction

1.1 What is problem-based learning?

Read the following text carefully.

A warm summer's day
It is a warm, muggy summer's day. If you look carefully you can see great
quantities of dust particles rising in the air. Towards the end of the afternoon,
dark clouds start to appear and the weather becomes even more oppressive. Then
there's a flash of lightning in the distance followed by a clap of thunder. Suddenly it starts to rain heavily.
Discuss these phenomena.

If you were presented with this problem as a student and stopped to think for a
minute about the sequence of events described, your train of thought might go
something like this:

'I think it's probably something to do with the causes of a thunderstorm. Static electricity is involved. Sparks bouncing off clouds of varying charges, i.e.
voltage, cause the flashes of lightning described in the problem. These flashes
are accompanied by a loud bang. This is probably due to the displacement of
different air pockets, which are first pressed together and then expand. But why
do these air pockets get pressed together? No idea. Of course, seeing the flash
of lightning before hearing the thunderclap is because light travels faster than
sound. Perhaps when air is moist it becomes a better conductor of electrical
current, but I'm not really sure why this should lead to a difference of charges
in the clouds. It's probably something to do with the temperature. Of course,
thunderstorms are more common in the summer, particularly late summer
when the air is warm and muggy, than in winter. They usually occur in the late
afternoon. Maybe it has something to do with those rising dust particles in the
air, but I'm not at all sure what part they play. Why do these particles rise?
Perhaps this is due to the heat convection from the earth's surface. I really don't
know. And how do the clouds receive an electrical charge?'

If you could think along these lines, it would seem that you had some prior
knowledge about the phenomena that you had been asked to explain. You know
something about static electricity, about the causes of a thunderclap, about the
different speeds at which light and sound travel through the air, and about the
conditions in which a thunderstorm is most likely to occur. You might also be

able to speculate about other aspects of the problem. But probably certain things really are beyond your comprehension. For example, what part is played by the rising dust particles, and how do clouds receive an electrical charge?
Did this come to *your* mind, thinking about the problem? Possibly you know more about the subject than the fictitious 'you' introduced above. Maybe you've managed to acquire more knowledge about the subject or you're just better at establishing links between the few things you do know and the text of the problem. But, if you wanted to tackle the problem in depth and you're not a meteorologist, no doubt you would engage yourself in the processes that cause a thunderstorm. In engaging yourself, and failing to find reasonable explanations, you might even develop a need to find out more about the processes to enable you to explain the problem better at a later stage.

This example represents the necessary ingredients of an educational method called *problem-based learning* (PBL). These ingredients are: a *problem description,* which invites further active deliberation; *prior knowledge* that is activated by the process of thinking through the problem; *questions* raised by the problem and the need – or *motivation* – to look for further information relevant to the problem at hand. When other students, who are also interested in the problem, *share* in the process of active deliberation and all this takes place *under the guidance of a tutor*, the essential elements of problem-based learning are in place. The remainder of this first chapter will discuss how these elements are built upon to form an approach to instruction that is definitely different from conventional lecture-based education.

Let's begin by explaining problem-based learning in the context of a course or curriculum. In problem-based learning, students are brought together in small tutorial groups of about six to ten peers. During their first meeting they are confronted with *the problem* as the starting point of the learning process, even before they are presented with any course material in the form of textbooks. The problem always comes first! They are expected to discuss the problem under the guidance of a *tutor*. Initially the group will produce a *tentative analysis* of the problem based on their prior knowledge, similar to the analysis conducted in the first paragraph of this book. This tentative analysis will lead to questions about issues not understood, clarified, or explained initially. These questions will be used by the students as *learning objectives* for *self-study*. In the period that elapses before the next tutorial – usually a few days – students will work towards these learning goals, either individually or in groups, by reading books and articles, watching video tapes, consulting teaching staff etc. Following this self-study phase, the students *report back* to each other in the tutorial, sharing what they have learned and evaluating the extent to which they have attained a better understanding of the problem through their self-study.

Problem-based instruction is usually organised in a number of *modules* (or courses), each of which dealing with a particular *theme* for a number of weeks.

These modules are arranged sequentially to form a curriculum. It is the job of the teachers responsible for the module to compile a *module book* to be used by students as a guide to negotiating their way through the subject matter. The module book consists of a number of problems, which offer the student a way of unravelling the module's main theme. The module book may also contain a short introduction to the theme, timetables, tutorial group lists, a list of learning resources (including literature, audio-visual aids and computer programmes), as well as a summary of supplementary study activities, such as practical work, lectures, excursions and skills training. A module book is *not* a syllabus, but indicates the *way* the related contents of a particular theme can be learned without actually containing any of the subject matter itself.

Problem-based learning was first introduced in 1969 at the medical school of McMaster University in Hamilton, Canada, and has been gaining popularity ever since. Universities and colleges throughout the world are now using it as the main educational method for courses in many subjects.
In the Netherlands, problem-based learning was first introduced in 1974 in the faculty of medicine at Maastricht University. Other faculties within this university have since adopted this method of teaching, e.g. law, economic sciences, psychology, humanities and health sciences. Problem-based learning has been adopted by other universities and colleges in a wide range of disciplines, such as engineering, nursing studies, and teacher training. Presently, about 500 curricula worldwide use problem-based learning.

The founding fathers of problem-based learning have suggested that the most important potential *benefits* of the method are: that students learn to analyse and solve the relevant problems of their domain of study, that they acquire knowledge that is retained over long stretches of life and can also be actually used; and that students develop the necessary self-directed skills for life-long learning. These potential benefits can only be achieved if the student adopts an active attitude to learning. This implies inquisitiveness about the problems associated with the theme, harnessing knowledge already acquired and gaining new knowledge and skills through in-depth analysis of the subject matter. Learning – that is the acquisition, retention and recall of knowledge – within a specific context and related to particular problems is more effective than the acquisition of facts and information simply gleaned by reading a book from cover to cover.

Problem-based learning assumes that the student is able to study independently, without being constantly spoon-fed by a teacher. This emphasis on self-directed learning demands discipline on the part of the students. For example, students will have to dig deeper and wider for study material, learn to distinguish the relevant from the trivial, plot out an individual course of study, consult fellow students and teachers, and explain to fellow students what they have learned themselves.

Of course, teachers have their role to play too. They are required to present the subject matter so that students can access the subject matter effectively. They are required to guide students though the subject matter in easy-to-follow ways and to establish a clear link between the various areas of study. In the tutorial, they enable students to learn and to collaborate. In addition, teachers are responsible for assessing the achievements of their students appropriately.

1.2 What is learning about?

To understand how problem-based learning works, it may be useful to know a little bit more about learning in general. Therefore in this paragraph we introduce four ideas crucial to understanding what learning is all about: (1) learning as the construction of meaning, (2) elaboration, (3) learning in context, and (4) intrinsic motivation as a motor for learning.

Learning as the construction of meaning. For a long time, educational theorists maintained that learning is essentially a *passive* process. The mind of the learner is a blank slate on which the teacher writes the knowledge. Knowledge acquisition in this view is essentially the same as filling an empty space. The learner listens as the teacher, or the book, does its work. If the student is paying sufficient attention, learning will automatically result. This theory has been the basis of much classroom instruction. However, it has difficulty explaining why students sometimes remember what they've learned quite differently from what they've been taught, as every teacher who has to mark exams can tell you. In addition, this theory cannot explain why many students have difficulty studying and remembering a text such as the following:

'Nobody tells productions when to act; they wait until conditions are ripe and then activate themselves. By contrast, chefs in the other kitchens merely follow orders. Turing units are nominated by their predecessors, von Neumann operations are all prescheduled, and LISP functions are invoked by other functions. Production system teamwork is more laissez-faire: each production acts on its own, when and where its private conditions are satisfied. There is no central control, and individual productions never directly interact. All communication and influence is via patterns in the common workspace – like anonymous 'to whom it may concern' notices on a public bulletin board.' [1]

Ordinary people experience difficulty understanding this text and blame it on the way it is phrased. The text is considered 'incoherent', 'difficult', or a 'collection of sentences put together in an arbitrary way'. However, not everyone would feel this way. Computer science students, for instance, would have no difficulty recognising that the writer is attempting to characterise different programming approaches in a somewhat informal way. They are able to do so because they have the *prior knowledge* (knowledge of Turing units, Von Neumann operations,

1 Haugeland, J. (1985). For more information see References.

LISP functions, etc.) enabling them to interpret the text appropriately. This fact and many others have led researchers to believe that learning is not a passive process; it is not filling empty spaces, but a process by which *the learner uses prior knowledge to construct meaning*. This theory has many implications, the most important being that knowledge cannot be transmitted automatically from teacher to learner. Learning requires an act of interpretation by the learner, using whatever knowledge he or she already possesses of the topic at hand. If the person does not possess sufficient prior knowledge, learning cannot take place. In addition: those who have more prior knowledge will profit more from new learning experiences. And thirdly: prior knowledge needs to be activated by the learning situation in order to be helpful in new learning.

Elaboration. Having sufficient prior knowledge and having this knowledge activated by the learning situation are in themselves not enough for new learning to take place. Prior knowledge helps in the initial interpretation of new knowledge to be acquired, it helps to *understand*, but for new information to become anchored in the brain more effort is necessary. *Repetition* of the new knowledge is a much-used strategy. For instance, when English speakers in French class have to learn the French word for 'sea' ('la mer'), they resort to rehearsing both words a number of times in the hope that the French equivalent persists in memory. However, a far more effective strategy is *elaboration*. 'To elaborate' means literally 'to work out' and consists of the enrichment of the relationship between two ideas with other related ideas. For instance, if one already knows that in French 'la mère' is 'the mother,' then this knowledge can be used to construct a relationship between the sea and la mer. This can for instance be accomplished by remembering that during your holidays in France last summer your mother was swimming in the sea: 'La mère nages dans (swims in) la mer.' Thus, by elaborating upon the relationship between two knowledge elements with the help of existing knowledge, stable facts will emerge in memory that are quite resistant to forgetting. Another example. The same applies to understanding and remembering the relationship between 'movement' and 'force' in physics. Many people believe that if an object moves it must contain a force that propels it forward, much like a driving car that moves over a highway thanks to its running engine. If there is no force (no 'engine'), the object will not move. Newtonian physics, however, assumes that once set into motion, an object needs no force to move on forever as long as there is no countervailing force such as gravity or friction. What helps in understanding this, is imagining that stopping the engine of a moving car does not stop the car. Despite the absence of a propelling force, the car continues to move forward, until road friction or brakes stop it. So, by elaborating on the relationship between force and movement through the example of the driving car, your memory constructs knowledge structures that turn out to be quite resistant to forgetting. Knowledge acquired this way has been demonstrated to be better usable.

Learning in context. A third element of learning is that people learn better in a meaningful context. Knowledge remains abstract as long as you only talk about 'movement,' 'force,' and 'inclined planes'. But as soon as a concrete context is invoked, such as a car driving on a highway, learning is facilitated. It is generally believed that learning in the context of situations relevant to the application of what is to be learned encourages the *transfer* of knowledge: Knowledge can be more easily applied. In medical education for instance, learning of medical knowledge is fostered if it can be done through confrontation with real (or simulated) patients.

Intrinsic motivation. A fourth element important to learning is intrinsic motivation. (Motivation is the *will* to learn.) Psychologists assume that there are two main forms of motivation: motivation driven by (1) extrinsic factors and (2) intrinsic motivation. If you are extrinsically motivated to learn, you are not that interested in the subject to be studied, but study in the first place because you expect a *reward*, for instance a 'pass' on your exam, or a high salary when you've graduated. You are intrinsically motivated if you study because the topic at hand does interest you in itself. For instance, you would read this particular book anyway, even if no examination followed.

Proponents of problem-based learning suggest that acquiring knowledge through working on problems in small groups will foster learning, because such an approach enables the processes mentioned here. (1) The initial discussion of a problem helps in activating relevant prior knowledge, thus facilitating the comprehension of subsequently studied new information on the problem. Problem discussion would therefore add to the construction of knowledge. (2) Discussing a problem and discussing the subject matter acquired through self-directed learning is known to be a good way of elaborating on a particular topic that leads to the establishment of knowledge structures in the mind that are more resistant to forgetting and thus more usable. (3) The situation of a problem is the context in which new learning takes place and (4) problem-based learning has been shown to increase intrinsic motivation.

1.3   Learning from and with each other

Problem-based learning means that although much of the work has to be done on your own, you will also be working with other students. It both recognises and highlights the interactive or collaborative aspects of learning. In your tutorial group, fellow students can make additional information resources available, come up with new ideas for explaining the problem-at-hand, and suggest alternative resources, which you might have overlooked on your own.
You can learn a great deal from your peers, not least because of the mixed nature of the group, which will vary according to age, gender, experience and interpersonal skills. This does not necessarily mean that students will always agree

with each other. Discussions will arise occasionally in which issues will be hotly contested. Different interpretations of the same information may emerge and different theories of the same phenomena will lead to healthy competition in the tutorial group. These differences of opinion regarding the subject matter actually aid learning. By expressing personal opinions, through arguing, through asking questions, and through the confrontation with someone else's ideas, students are actively involved in the subject and are likely to enrich their knowledge. Where differences in personal and social ideas occur and are discussed in the context of instruction, it becomes possible to shed light on an individual student's perspective by comparing it with alternative standpoints.

Learning from and with each other in a tutorial group assumes a willingness of all those taking part to work actively together. The success of a tutorial can only be achieved if every member of the group is prepared to contribute something towards it. Tutorials where students merely attend for their own personal gain are unlikely to prosper. Tolerance of the views of others by participants is another important facet of the tutorial. It is also important for the tutorial to follow certain working procedures. These procedures will be dealt with in greater detail in subsequent chapters.

1.4   What do we know about the effectiveness of problem-based learning?[2]

Often, students are exposed to educational technologies that have never been scientifically studied. For instance, lecturing, certainly the most used mode of teaching in higher education, has hardly ever been studied, and not much is presently known about its effectiveness. Since problem-based learning is a fairly new approach to learning and instruction, its proponents have faced scepticism and rejection by those favouring more conventional methods of teaching. The scepticism of these opponents has encouraged much research. Let's briefly summarise what we know about the effects of problem-based learning. The findings displayed first are all based on comparisons between problem-based and conventional curricula.

First, students in problem-based curricula enjoy their education far more than students in similar conventional curricula; they think their training is more relevant to their future professional life; they prefer working in small groups more than attending lectures, they report less stress, fewer feelings of being powerless, and less fatalism, and feel more supported by their learning environment.[3]

---

2   Unlike most of the other sections in this book, this one contains references. Inclusion of references here enables teachers and students who wish to know more about research on problem-based learning to find appropriate resources. One interesting overall resource is: Schmidt, H. G. & Moust, J. H. C. (2000). For more information see References.
3   Kiessling, C., Schubert, B., Scheffner, D., & Burger, W. (2004). Ibid

Second, in Dutch national surveys comparing the quality of higher education, problem-based curricula always end up first or second in their category.[4] Third, graduates from problem-based schools report that they consider themselves better equipped in interpersonal competencies, such as teamwork, consulting with clients, and leadership. In addition, they consider themselves more independent, more creative and more efficient in their work.[5] And fourth, they display better problem-solving skills than students from conventional programs,[6] although they do not have more profession-specific knowledge.[7]

The second source of our knowledge about problem- based learning comes from experiments. A representative study was conducted by De Grave, Schmidt, and Boshuizen.[8] They presented groups of medical students with a problem about blood circulation. The students in the 'experimental' groups first discussed this problem and subsequently studied a problem-relevant physiology text. The other 'control' groups of students discussed an irrelevant problem (about perception) and then studied the same text as the experimental groups. The knowledge acquired from the text was tested in both sets of groups. The set who had discussed a relevant problem prior to studying the text gained a much higher test score, indicating that they had learned more from the same text.

In summary, research findings suggest that problem-based learning facilitates learning, makes learning more interesting, and provides a learning environment that is more student-friendly. In addition, problem-based learning fosters the development of profession-relevant competencies in graduates. These are all good reasons to give problem-based learning a serious try.

1.5   Problem-based learning in an electronic environment

Electronic work stations are increasingly being used in support of educational processes. In its simplest form students are offered e-mail facilities and the learning materials are presented on the internet. More advanced systems support the work of students outside the tutorial group by offering options to post findings and to comment on findings offered by others. And obviously sophisticated tools like lab simulations, video presentations and graphic tools can be linked to text materials. Electronic learning environments provide good opportunities to make a clear end product, such as a concluding short report, with links to underpinning electronic notes and other documentation. To work effectively you have to fully explore the possibilities of the system in use. It's important to regularly check

---

4 Keuzegids Hoger Onderwijs 2006-2007: Verzamelgids. (Consumer Report Higher Education 2006-2007). (2006). Ibid
5 Schmidt, H.G., Vermeulen, L., & Van der Molen, H.T. (2006). Ibid
6 Schuwirth, L.W., Verhoeven, B.H., Scherpbier, A.J., Mom, E.M., Cohen-Schotanus, J., Van Rossum, H.J., (1999). Ibid
7 Van der Vleuten, C.P.M., Schuwirth, L.W.T., Muijtens, A.M.M., Thoben, A.J.N.M., Cohen-Schotanus, J., & Van Boven, C.P.A. (2004). Ibid
8 De Grave, W.S., Schmidt, H.G., & Boshuizen, H.P.A. (2001). Ibid

your deadlines for the work to be done in order to contribute well to the group result. Learning how to use an electronic work environment is also a good preparation for your professional career since similar systems are used to coordinate work processes in many fields.

1.6　Skills in problem-based learning

Now let's look briefly at the skills necessary for students to get the most out of problem-based learning.

It is important to recognise the major differences between secondary and higher education. The latter distinguishes itself from the former in the following areas:
- the amount of subject matter to be mastered is more extensive;
- the material is usually more demanding;
- teachers check less frequently if the student has grasped the subject matter;
- students are more often left to work on their own initiative;
- the subject matter may be presented in another language (in countries where English is not the first language).

When the concept of problem-based learning is introduced, the following points also apply:
- the subject matter is often not dealt with on a subject-by-subject or book-by-book basis, but is provided in the form of problems of a multidisciplinary or integrated nature;
- greater demands are placed on students to work on their own initiative. They are expected to analyse problems for themselves, set their own learning goals and search the literature for themselves;
- students must be able to work together in small group tutorials.

This book deals with three types of skills that are essential to the concept of problem-based learning:
1　skills necessary to deal with problems in a methodological manner;
2　skills necessary to conduct individual learning activities;
3　skills necessary to function successfully in small groups.

Chapter 2 focuses on the process of problem-based learning in detail, elucidating the strategies that can be used when working on a range of different types of problems. Chapter 3 concentrates on working in the tutorial as well as discussing communication within the group and the different roles played out in the tutorial. It pays particular attention to the respective roles of the chair (the leader of the discussion), the scribe and the tutor. Chapter 4 looks at individual study skills with the emphasis on study activities essential to problem-based learning e.g. identifying sources of literature, studying these, and setting up a documentation system. Chapter 5 discusses the skills that need to be mastered in order to function well within the tutorial group, including aspects such as the exchange of information, listening and summarising skills and evaluating tutorial group meetings. Chapter 6 focuses on the responsibilities of the group's chair during the phases of both analysis and synthesis as well as on improving collaboration between the members of a tutorial group.

Chapters 5 and 6 also offer appendices presenting various observation schemes and questionnaires useful for self-reflection and feedback from peers as well as tutors.

2   Learning through problems

2.1   Introduction

As we argued in the first chapter, learning in problem-based learning always
involves a confrontation with a problem. Problems serve both as the context and
focus for learning. A problem makes learning concrete – it is better to imagine a
particular patient with a name and a history whose complaints one has to understand than merely study the causes of a disease; it is more useful to deal with the
causes of the drought in a specific ecosystem such as the Sahel in Africa than
to study desertification in the abstract. In addition, learning through problems
helps you understand *why* you are studying. It makes clear that the knowledge
you acquire is not to be mastered only because of an examination, but because
you *need* that knowledge to be able to understand and solve concrete problems
in your future professional life. In this chapter, we introduce you to the various
types of problems that are used in problem-based learning and to the ways you
will deal with these problems. In close collaboration with your peers, you will
learn how to translate a problem into a set of learning goals that can be used for
independent learning.

2.2   Various types of problems for problem-based learning

In tutorials, *problems* mark the starting point of the learning process. Problems
are designed by teachers to be analysed and discussed in the tutorial group. Discussing the problems leads to the formulation of learning goals, the selection of
specific literature for further study, and the preparation of reports for subsequent
tutorials. Problems form the basis of the module book. In some ways a module
book can be compared to a railway timetable in that during the module the
learning activities help you get from A to B. In addition to problems, the module
book usually introduces the subject matter, provide timetables for practical work
and presentations, and suggests sources for further reading.
Problems are not always structured identically and may be presented in such
forms as case descriptions, study assignments, and literature quotes. Sometimes
the module book indicates ways in which the problems can best be tackled but,
generally, it will be the tutorial group itself that decides on how the work should
be carried out.

To be effective, it is essential to work on the problems in a *systematic* fashion.
Members of the tutorial group need to structure their activities so that they are
working towards a specific *result*. By 'result' we do not necessarily mean solving
the problem per se, but rather acquiring knowledge and gaining insight into the

diverse aspects of the subject matter covered by the problem. The problem-based method of working should lead to a better understanding and new knowledge related to the original problem.

Various types of problems can be identified, each requiring a different approach. This chapter presents the composition of these problems and examines the approaches required for them. We will first look at the following types of problems: explanation problems, strategy problems, dilemma problems. Subsequently we will offer other types of problems and alternative approaches to discussing problems in a tutorial group.

2.3   Explanation problems

In educational settings, explanation problems are usually set in the form of a *description of a number of phenomena that appear to be related in some way and for which the students are expected to find an underlying explanation.* To track down these explanations, the tutorial group members have to find out what mechanisms, processes or structures, ideas and rules are relevant. The aim is to understand how these phenomena relate to each other. This understanding forms the key to professional expertise in any particular discipline.

Problems can be formulated for numerous subjects and at several levels of human functioning, e.g. a cell, an organ, an individual, a group or an organisational level. The way in which the problems are presented can vary. For example, the presentation might consist of a written or visualised description of a situation, a graph or a photograph with an accompanying assignment, a transcription of a conversation between a client and a professional advisor or quotes taken from a newspaper article. In some problems, additional information may be provided while the problem is being examined. This information may be supplementary to the module book and may be provided directly by the tutor.

Boxes 1, 2 and 3 provide examples of explanation problems from various disciplines.

Box 1 *Example of an explanation problem in medicine*

> *Sudden weight gain: A normal process when you are over forty?*
> A man in his forties comes to your office complaining that he has grown fat in a short time. His abdomen is so swollen he finds it difficult to fasten his belt. His eyelids and the skin around his eyes appear to be swollen too. The percentage of plasma protein in his blood is lower than normal.

Box 2 *Example of an explanation problem in the health sciences*

> *The French paradox*
> Many consider France a paradise on earth. This is partly because of the lusty appetite of the French for all the good things in life. A glass of wine and a well-

stocked dinner table are integral parts of the French culinary tradition.
France is one of the great wine-producing countries in the world. Wine consumption in France is the highest worldwide. High alcohol consumption is often seen as an unhealthy habit. Health indicators are in line with this fact: The French suffer from high levels of liver cirrhosis. However, epidemiological studies show that France has no higher mortality rates than other countries in the west. In particular, the French don't succumb more often to cardiovascular diseases, number one killer in the western world, despite the fact that they show higher values that indicate health risks in this area. The French not only drink more, they also consume more animal fats. They display on average higher cholesterol levels and higher blood pressure. They smoke more and don't exercise as much as other nationalities. Despite these higher health risk indicators, in particular for cardiovascular disease, fewer French people die of diseases of the heart than people anywhere else.

Box 3 *Example of an explanation problem in economics*

Market mechanisms in the Maastricht[9] pub scene
Although Maastricht landlords claim there's little competition between pubs in town, in reality competition is fierce. Turnover is considerable. The main square, the Vrijthof, houses many expensive pubs but since people seem to think the expense is worthwhile for the atmosphere the pavement cafes are always crowded. In the surrounding streets and squares, the pub prices are generally lower, but if you fancy a cheap beer then you'll have to find a back-street pub. In many cases, the price of beer seems more expensive than marginal costs, but that doesn't necessarily mean that every pub landlord makes a profit, even those on the Vrijthof.

2.4   The seven-step method of working with explanation problems

A tutorial group will provide an excellent forum for working with problems as long as it adopts the right approach. If the group chooses to tackle problems aimlessly, it will waste a lot of time. To save time, we have developed a working method, which we call the *seven-step method* (or *'seven-leap'* as it was originally called). The seven-step method was specially devised for tackling problems. As the name suggests, the method consists of seven steps through which a tutorial group must progress to maximise learning from a problem. The seven steps are summarised in box 4 and are discussed individually using two examples: a meteorology problem ('A warm summer's day') and a psychological problem ('Who am I?'). The problems are explained in boxes 5 and 6. Perhaps it's an

9   Maastricht, a city in the south of the Netherlands, is home to its first, entirely problem-based learning university.

idea to start thinking up some explanations for the phenomena described in these problems before you read the text carefully. Thinking about these explanations will give you a bit of practice with the problem-based learning approach. To give you an impression of the various stages involved in the seven-step method, we will present several excerpts of a discussion of one of these problems taking place in a fictitious tutorial group.

Box 4 *The seven-step method*

Step 1. Clarify unclear terms and concepts in the problem text
Step 2. Define the problem: What exactly needs explaining?
Step 3. Problem analysis: Produce as many ideas as possible
Step 4. Problem analysis: Arrange the ideas systematically and analyse them in-depth
Step 5. Formulate learning goals
Step 6. Seek information from learning resources
Step 7. Synthesise and apply the new information

Box 5 *Example of an explanation problem in meteorology*

A warm, summer's day
Early one morning you go biking with your friends on the heath near Maastricht. Contrary to the weather forecast it becomes a warm, muggy day. When you look carefully you can see great quantities of dust particles rising in the air. Towards the end of the afternoon, dark clouds start forming in the welkin. Everybody complains about the muggy weather. There is a flash of lightning in the far distance followed by a clap of thunder. Suddenly it starts raining heavily. Flashes of lightning and thunderclaps come in rapid succession. Desperately you look around for some safe shelter.

Box 6 *Example of an explanation problem in psychology*

Who am I?
On September 3, 1979 some 8,000 people were waiting to be admitted to a concert of British rock band *The Who* at the Riverfront Coliseum in Cincinnati. The queue in front of the small entrance doors was long, and when the doors opened and people heard the band doing a sound check, the crowd exploded. People on the outside began pushing in to the middle, causing the fans in front to be crushed. People fainted, were pushed aside, and fell onto the concrete floor. The crowd saw only the open doors and heard the music. The imperturbable mass pushed its way to the entrance, ignoring those being crushed under their feet. Eleven people died, many were injured.

Step 1: Clarify unclear terms and concepts

The first thing to do when faced with a problem is to clear up any uncertainties in the text. This will enable all tutorial group members to understand the content of the information.

The above examples are relatively easy to understand. The situations have been described briefly and concisely without going into detail about the history and evolution of the problems. They contain no difficult psychological or meteorological terms. Later on in courses, the problems given tend to become more complex and often contain more professional jargon.

Whilst problems may take no more space than a few lines, a description of the situation arising from the problems might take up several pages. In such cases, you should first take the time to check if everyone understands the terms and concepts used in the problem and in the description of the situation. More often than not, the prior knowledge of some group members will help clarify matters. During the first step, everybody agrees on the interpretation of the various terms in the description of the problem. This means that there should be no conflicting interpretations.

Finally, the group might want to agree on the boundaries of their studies or to exclude specific aspects of the problem. Doing this provides a precisely defined frame of reference from which group members are not expected to deviate.

During the first step of the seven-step method, we identify three activities:
1 ensure that everyone understands the terminology;
2 ensure that everyone sees the situation described in the same way with no ambiguity;
3 ensure that everyone agrees on aspects that are beyond the remit of the problem.

Box 7 offers an example of step 1.

Box 7 *Example of step 1: Clarification of unclear terms or concepts in the text of a problem*

Chair: Has everybody read the problem? Okay. Are any of the terms or concepts not clear?

Jane: What does welkin mean?

Tom: The atmosphere, I think.

Sarah: It's an archaic word used mostly by poets. We use it for sky, so presumably atmosphere is correct.

Chair: Okay, let's define welkin tentatively as the sky. At home we can look it up in a dictionary to see if that's correct. Any other problems with this text? (Looks around) None? Is the described situation clear to everybody? (No further reactions) Okay, shall we go on with the definition of the problem?

Step 2: Define the problem

The second step in the seven-step is to define the problem precisely. The group must agree on which phenomena require an explanation and on the relationships that exist between them.

Sometimes, the problem is clear right from the start. Everyone can identify its central issue. If this is the case, you can proceed to step 3. However, in some descriptions the relationships between phenomena are not always clear and subordinate problems might complicate matters. Sometimes the problem can be looked at from a number of different angles. If this is the case, take time to categorise the information and come to some kind of collective agreement on how to proceed. The problem-definition step is not always easy. Often the information has to be seen in the context of the subject. For example, with a medical problem, you would need to look at the indications and symptoms whereas for a legal problem you would have to identify the parties involved and the relationships between them. It might be useful to set out the key issues and the relationships between them in a diagram.

Box 8 shows an example of step 2.

Box 8 *Example of step 2: Define the problem*

Chair: Shall we go on with the definition of the problem? What phenomena need explaining?

Anne: How does a thunderstorm develop?

Eva: More specifically, what makes lightning happen? And the thunderclap, of course.

Paul: Another problem seems to me how people can protect themselves from thunderstorms.

Chair: Anybody else? (Looks around) Nobody? Okay, I suggest we have two main questions. First, what makes a thunderstorm and, more specifically, the phenomena of lightning and a thunderclap? The second main question is: how can people protect themselves against the dangers of a thunderstorm? I suggest that we start by brainstorming briefly to pool our ideas and our existing knowledge of these topics.

Step 3: Problem analysis: Produce as many ideas as possible

Having read through the text and attempted to see the problem as broadly as possible, you will soon begin conjuring up all sorts of ideas and assumptions. These ideas about how the problem is structured will be based on your existing knowledge or may be a result of thinking through the problem logically.

The group's analysis of the problem now consists of finding out what the various group members think or know (or believe they know) about the problem's underlying processes and mechanisms. At this point the group will not just limit itself to discussing factual information but will also try to formulate possible *explana-*

tions on the basis of common sense. In this process, it is essential for each group member to be given an opportunity to make a short contribution before you go on to examine the ideas and assumptions more critically. That's more easily said than done. What often happens when someone puts forward an idea is that others interrupt, make additional points or simply criticise the idea. The person with the original idea may react in a number of ways. For example, by impulsively defending his or her position without regard for what the others have to say, or conversely, by backing down and withdrawing from the rest of the tutorial. Such reactions might result in a restricted discussion, with important information being omitted.

Brainstorming is a technique that can help avoid these communication difficulties. When you are brainstorming, it is essential to bear specific rules in mind. These rules will help effective discussion of a wide spectrum of knowledge and ideas. The *basic rule* of brainstorming is that *generating ideas is separate from the critical analysis of those ideas.*

A brainstorming session begins by allowing everyone to have a good think and to jot down any keywords they can come up with. Following this, group members briefly report their opinions and knowledge about the problem. Some may make categorical statements, whilst others may only be able to put forward undeveloped ideas. In most cases, inadequate knowledge of a particular problem will prevent you from explaining the problem fully at this stage. Each member of the group will be asked to make a contribution in turn. Group members should be given the chance to intervene when a relevant idea occurs to them but try to avoid clashes over differing ideas at this stage. Whenever possible, reactions should be limited to clarifying questions. There will be further opportunities to agree the relative merits of the information later on in the tutorial.

It may be useful to note down the ideas brought up, listing a number of keywords on the board. The note-taker or scribe can do this.

Box 9 provides a fragment of the initial analysis of the same problems used above.

Box 9 *Example of step 3: Problem analysis. A fragment of the brainstorming session on 'A warm summer's day'*

Chair:	Now, let's start the brainstorming session. First, has anybody an idea about what causes lightning?
Jane:	A far as I know it has something to do with electricity, with differences in charges, electric sparks jumping between the clouds and the earth.
John:	I thought it has to do with the friction between the clouds.
Tom:	I read somewhere that it's all about static electricity. Differences in potentials inside a cloud.
Chair:	Anyone else? (Silence). No one, so far. Let's think about the causes of thunder.
Sarah:	In the olden days people used to think the sound was made by an angry god out riding his chariot and horses through the clouds…
(Everybody laughs)	

Anne:	I think that air gets displaced. Air expands due to the heat of the lightning. The clouds bump into each other and that results in an explosion of sound.
Chair:	Other ideas?
Jane:	I think lightning makes a hole through the clouds. Then the clouds roll back. That explains thunder.
Chair:	So, Anne says it's an explosion of clouds, while Jane sticks to the idea of implosion. Anyone else? (Looks around). Nobody, then let's brainstorm on the second problem, how to be safe when there's lightning,
Jane:	If there are trees around you can always shelter under them. You only have to keep far enough away from the trunk.
Peter:	I thought it was better to go out into the open.
Paul:	Yes, but you'd have to crouch down low.
Jane:	Yes, lightning always seeks out the highest object, so what you're suggesting is dangerous.
Chair:	Anyone else? (Looks around, nobody reacts). Okay, now let's we explore our ideas in more depth. Shall we look at we've got on the blackboard?

Box 10 *Example of step 3: Problem analysis. A fragment of the brainstorming session on 'Who am I?'*

Chair:	Our task is to formulate as many ideas about the problem as we can come up with. How could human beings trample other humans to death under the circumstances described in the problem? Who would like to say something about it?
Gino:	It could have been an accident. But I don't believe that's the case here. Those people wanted to see The Who so badly, they forgot about anything else. If you want something that badly, you tend to push everything else aside.
Anique:	Of course, and it would have been dark out there. That would make you anonymous to a large extent and perhaps then you'd feel less responsible for the fate of other people. Also there were so many people, most of whom you wouldn't know personally. I think this reinforces the sense of anonymity.
Peter:	No doubt those people were drunk and there you have it. People feel less responsible when they are intoxicated. If you're drunk, you lose your sense of what is appropriate and what is not. The norms and values you grew up with disappear.
Wilco:	You get swallowed up by the masses. You're no longer an individual. This also happens during Carnival or Mardi Gras. The mask you wear adds to the loss of individuality. You simply stop feeling responsible for your own behavior.

Step 4: Problem analysis: Arrange your ideas systematically and analyse them in depth

During this phase of problem analysis, the original ideas put forward by the group members are scrutinised in greater depth and sorted into some sort of systematic order. The process of *analysis,* i.e. the division of the whole into its constituent parts, involves identifying internal relationships, categorising the different elements by means of their mutual dependence, and separating relevant aspects from irrelevant ones. The first thing is to start *arranging* the ideas coming up during the brainstorm session. Ideas that appear similar are treated as an entity, whilst opposing viewpoints are recognised as such; possible explanations are arranged.

Once you have finished the *initial clustering,* those putting forward the ideas are asked to *elaborate* on what they have suggested. Then the group will examine any differences in opinion more closely and critically discuss and compare the ideas.

During this phase, individual group members should be given the freedom to express their ideas. Other group members can add to their own contributions, pose clarifying questions or expand on assumptions already made. Ambiguities will often occur during the discussion. Individuals won't necessarily understand the way in which everything is pieced together; contradictory explanations may have been given for a specific phenomenon; or new questions arise which cannot be answered directly. Such ambiguities and contradictions form the basis for Step 5 in which learning goals are formulated.

It is very tempting for students to try to take short cuts at this stage. It's not always an easy job to convince them of the importance of explaining the rationale behind their ideas or interpretations, but this deeper analysis is essential to find out what you collectively already know or think you know. By pooling the knowledge of the group, you will find it easier to understand any new information and it will help you to be more focussed when you search through the study material. By bringing to mind your prior knowledge, you will improve your ability to learn and store new information. In this phase of the analysis, it will become clear how much of the information has not yet been understood, where there are different interpretations within the group and where the counterarguments lie. This is a productive way of going about things. After all, if the problems could be explained in an instant, they wouldn't be given as the starting point for learning. It is the outstanding issues, the loose ends of discussion, the uncertainties and contradictory arguments that provide the gateway to the next phase of study. Box 11 provides an example of this process.

Box 11 *Example of step 4: Problem analysis. A fragment of the session on systematic idea clustering and in-depth analysis of 'A warm summer's day'*

Chair:	Shall we see what's on the board? (Reads out loud the keywords noted down by the scribe)

Lightning: (static) electricity

                friction

                differences in potentiality

Thunder: displacement of air leads to explosion or implosion

Shelter: (not) under a tree, crouching down on the ground, do not lie down, transport lightning – tree – human body?

Okay, let us explore our ideas in more depth.

Let's go back to the causes of lightning. Some group members thought it had to do with electricity and friction. Jane, John, Tom you brought this up. Can you tell us more about this?

Tom: The lightning, you see, is sparks which short-circuits between the clouds themselves and between the clouds and earth. There is a difference in potential, ah, voltage? I think that the clouds grate on each other. That causes friction, ah, electric charge? When you rub a comb through your hair, you also get electricity. How does it go with that ebonite rod, plus or minus? Static electricity is the concept, I think…

Sarah: I don't understand how you get the potentials. Are clouds positive and negative?

Tom: Of course. That's why clouds collide. They pull together like magnets.

John: But, the differences in potential, doesn't that develop in the clouds? From above downwards? Lightning usually happens in summer, when the earth is warm. Hot air rises and gradually cools down. But I don't understand how those clouds get charged? Clouds are made of raindrops, aren't they?

Eva: That's right, but those raindrops become ice. Thunderclouds can go up terrifically high and this makes the raindrops freeze and ice crystals develop. Those crystals of ice get sucked up by the upward turbulence. I think the difference in potential develops because ice crystals are in the higher layers of the clouds and water particles are in the layers underneath. At the top of the clouds there is a positive charge and at the bottom a negative one. The lightning develops between these two charges.

Paul: … Um, but how do you explain the lightning across clouds and also between the clouds and earth?

Eva: I don't know exactly….

Anne: Perhaps the humidity in the air supports the conductivity of electricity. But where are the plus and minus charges exactly? And what charge does the earth have: plus or minus?

Tom: Minus. There always is a current from the clouds to the earth and visa versa. There must be a balance between the atmosphere and earth. Perhaps lightning has some role in this process?

Chair: I'm hearing many different theories. Potential differences either in or between clouds, a partial description of the process which gives electricity, a possible relation between lightning and the electric current between the earth and the atmosphere.

Scribe: I heard once that there are lots of thunderstorms in the tropics and that those storms serve a useful interaction between the earth and the atmosphere. Both entities have differences in potentiality which can't just go on and on without end. Now and then there must be, um, some sort of exchange. Lightning contributes to this process. But how?

(Silence)

Chair: I get the feeling that these are our initial ideas? (Looks around, nobody reacts. Looks at the board where the scribe has drawn a scheme based on the remarks.) Okay, let me try to summarise what we have so far. We suppose that hot air rises. At a high level the air cools down. This results in condensation and freezing which creates ice crystals and fosters differences in electric potentiality. We also mentioned something about severe turbulence. And that lightning seems to be playing a role in the balance between earth and atmosphere. We've also had lots of questions. Our scribe has written down some of the important ones, such as, how does electricity develop in clouds? Where are the differences in charge? Is the earth plus or minus? What is the specific relationship between the earth and atmosphere? Does anybody want to add more information?

(Silence)

Chair: Okay. Well, let's discuss the thunder. Somebody thought that has to do with air displacement.

Sarah: Thunder always follows lightning. Lightning forces the air to displace. After the lightning the air falls down the hole that was developed by the lightning.

Anne: No, no! Clouds explode because the current of the lightning is very, very hot, they expand. At a certain moment these clouds collide with other cold clouds which have not expanded yet. That causes the thunder.

Paul: I had the idea that air must first get pressed together, then it expands later…

(The discussion goes on…)

Chair: (Summarises the various theories again, and presents an overview of the questions stated during the discussion.) Okay, let's discuss the last problem: how dangerous is lightning and how can we protect ourselves from it?

Jane:	Outside, it can be very dangerous. You can shelter under a tree if you keep some distance from the trunk.
Peter:	You do better walking out in the open.
Anne:	Yes, but you should lie down otherwise you'd be the highest point around.
Eva:	Whoa! That's seems dangerous to me too. Lying down, your body presents a long area. I've heard that cows, for instance, often get hit by lightning due to the fact that when they're stretched out they present a big area. The current goes in through their front legs and out through their back legs behind. It's very dangerous to lie down.
Peter:	Didn't Paul suggest that you should make yourself small, and crouch down low. Why is that?
Eva:	You should spread your legs a bit and stand on tiptoe so that you have less contact with the ground. And, please keep away from bikes or any other metal object.
Tutor:	That's strange. I once heard that you can best shelter in a car during a thunderstorm.
Eva:	That's a Faraday cage. I think. In this case the metal conducts the current to the earth.
Tom:	But the metal isn't in contact with the ground. Car tyres are made of rubber which is a bad conductor of electricity. Sometimes you see those earthing strips under a car, but that isn't it, or is it?
(Silence)	
Chair:	Let me briefly summarise. (…) Okay, I suggest that we start formulating learning goals now. Various questions have been written on the blackboard during our analysis. Who wants to propose a learning objective?

Let's look at the brainstorming session of the 'Who am I?' problem analysed by the psychology students. According to these students, the trampling of people before The Who concert was caused by two psychological processes: loss of individuality and loss of norms. These processes, in turn, would result from the fact that it was dark when the incident occurred, that people may have been under the influence of alcohol, that a crowd had gathered, and that most people in the crowd didn't know each other. The board might therefore contain the inventory presented in box 12. This inventory arranges and summarises what has been produced during problem analysis.

Box 12 *Organization of brainstorm results for the 'Who am I?' problem*

Dusk Assumed alcohol use Other people are strangers	→	Loss of individuality Loss of norms	→ Trampling over people

Step 5: Formulate learning goals

Learning goals are formulated on the basis of questions raised when analysing the problem. These questions must be answered for the problem to be understood more easily. Learning goals can be considered *study assignments* that the tutorial group sets itself on the basis of the preceding discussion. They form the foundation for the study activities taking place between the present and the next tutorial meeting. For a tutorial to function well, it is important for learning goals to be established by group members reaching a consensus. These goals will serve as a starting point for the self-study phase. It's also very important for some individual learning goals to be set. After all, each student needs to master the study material independently and some students may have less experience and knowledge in certain areas. Just because the group decides that one particular aspect is not essential doesn't necessarily mean that you needn't look at it in closer detail yourself. It may help you with an area that you had been struggling with previously or hadn't come across before.

A lively tutorial meeting may result in a large number of learning goals being formulated. Usually, priorities will have to be set; otherwise it won't be possible to give complete consideration to the full scope of the problem. Therefore it is up to the group to decide on which aspects of the discussion they will focus on the next time. If this is the case, the group members should decide on how these learning goals can best be met. Groups are sometimes inclined to think that the work should be divided up, each member concentrating on one of the learning goals. If this approach is adopted, students report back on their own specific task at the next meeting and everyone is asked to express an opinion. This type of tutorial becomes more a series of monologues than an active discussion of the issues and holds a number of other disadvantages as well. Primarily, individuals expected to work together have no common ground on which to interact. Everyone is a specialist in a specific topic and this hampers constructive discussion. Moreover, this method of cooperation is limited to only a few possible outcomes, such as a reference to a book or a fragmentary summary of what has been read. This style of tutorial can put success at serious risk if one of the students happens to be absent from the tutorial or has not done what was expected. It means that a piece of the jigsaw is missing and that will hamper progress. Equally, nobody can check the authenticity of the information provided by an individual group member with any confidence. That individual will have become the authority in the group regarding that particular aspect, with the result that anything they say is assumed to be true. So, dividing up learning goals amongst the students clearly has disadvantages and should be avoided as much as possible. However, on occasion, this method can be useful, e.g. if the subject matter has so many aspects that each deserves further examination on its own. How can the risks associated with this way of working be minimised? Here are a number of suggestions:

- Whilst all students are expected to study the main aspects of the problem, the secondary aspects can be divided up amongst individual group members.
- The tutorial is split into two or more 'mini-groups', each concentrating on

one of the learning goals. Each mini-group should consist of at least three people, so that the accuracy of the information can be verified.
- The group does not separate out any of the learning goals, instead it agrees on who will consult which information sources (if these are known to the group).

At the beginning of a particular course, it will take some effort to formulate effective learning goals. No doubt, you will first have to get used to the idea of formulating questions, but it will help reinforce your learning process, even if you find it hard at first to grasp all the concepts in the field of study.

To reiterate: in problem-based learning, the main priority is not to solve the problem that has been set per se, but rather to acquire knowledge of issues within a particular field of study. The problems written by the teachers provide the main starting point from which to tackle the various aspects found within the module's recommended reading list. Learning goals, as such, go beyond simply solving a problem. In formulating questions and ideas, you will of course have to take into account the central issues presented by the module. Usually, the introductory section of the module book gives an indication of the most important principles, theories and fields of study. Learning goals form the bridge between the questions raised by analysing the problem and the information that can be acquired on the subject from various disciplines. For effective study, therefore, it is essential to formulate the learning goals so that they provide easy access to literature and other learning resources, such as educational videos or computer-assisted learning packages.

In our examples, the learning goals may be formulated as follows; see boxes 13 and 14.

Box 13 *Example of step 5: Formulation of learning goals derived from 'A warm summer's day'*

Chair:	Who wants to propose a learning objective?
Anne:	We should look up what welkin means.
Sarah:	What puzzles me is where the process of lightning starts and the role of electricity. Where are positive and negative currents, in or between the clouds? Is the earth plus or minus? We have Eva's theory about ice crystals and raindrops, but that doesn't explain everything. Our learning goal could be defined as: find out what the electrical process is in or between clouds. And, what is the role of ice crystals?
Peter:	We also don't have a clear theory about thunder. Is it an implosion or an explosion of the clouds? How does it work?
John:	And we want to know more about protection against lightning. Why is it so dangerous to stand under a tree? How would you protect yourself in the open? Or protect yourself inside a building? And what is a Faraday's cage, exactly?
Chair:	Let's not forget the question about the roles of thunder and lightning in the whole climatologic process.

(The scribe writes down the various learning objective on the board).

Box 14 *Example of step 5: Formulation of learning issues derived from
'Who am I?'*

- Why do people behave differently when in a crowd?
- Under which circumstances do people behave differently?
- What makes it possible for people to lose their sense of individuality in a crowd?
- What allows a decrease in norms and values?

Tutorial groups are sometimes inclined to be satisfied with vague, generalised learning goals. However, this will result in each member of the group being obliged to keep reformulating the goals on their own. A subsequent tutorial might reveal that different members of the group have been studying different things. Thus poorly formulated learning objectives lead to wasted time for group members, both during the tutorial and their individual studies. The point is that there is no reference point from which the contribution of new learning resources can be judged.

Step 6: Seeking additional information outside the group from other resources

Once the learning goals have been clearly formulated, you can start searching for information and studying them. Step 6 relates to the individual study activities performed between two tutorial meetings. Not all students tackle their studies in the same way. Numerous styles exist and they can all be used productively. These styles may include: drawing diagrams, comparing the views of different authors, making an in-depth examination of a particular problem, studying with the help of audio-visual aids, preferring to look at practical aspects of the problem.

In Chapter 4 of this book we discuss the selection and study of learning resources in more detail. Here, we restrict ourselves to specifying a number of points important to the concept of self-study.

- *Careful selection of learning resources.* Don't start by just reading a book in the hope that you will come across the required subject matter.
- *Active study.* When you are reading the material, e.g. keep asking yourself whether it puts you in a better position to answer the questions identified in the tutorial.
- *Try to summarise the learning resources in your own words.* It is pointless if the tutorial group simply regurgitates an author's text word for word as an answer to the learning objective. During your study, ask yourself the following: how can I best explain it to someone else, even if it concerns a question relating to a subject that I don't know much about.
- *Consult more than one source.* During your studies you will soon discover that the experts often differ in their opinions on the interpretation of phenomena.

- *Read around your learning goals.* It is not enough to simply look for the information that will give you a straightforward answer to the question. The problems set in the module book (and the accompanying learning goals) refer you to specific aspects of different fields of study. If you complete your work on the learning goals too quickly, it might mean you've not done enough.
- *Write down clearly the source of the information.* This is not only important when you report back to the tutorial group, but for yourself when you want to consult your notes again.
- *Make clear notes about the main points.*

Box 15 provides an overview of some learning resources students can study regarding the thunderstorm problem.

Box 15 *Example of step 6: Learning resources students consulted for 'A warm summer's day'*

- Uman, M.A (2001). The lightning discharge. Courier Dover Publication.
- Macgorman, D.R. & Rust, W.D. (1998). The electric nature of storms. Oxford University Press.
- Lightning protection from thunderstorm. www.britannica.com/eb/article218342/thunderstorm
- Kids' lightning Information and safety. www.kidslightning/info/zaphome/stm
- Lightning. Wikipedia – the free encyclopedia.
(Many resources can be found through Google, using such keywords as lightning, thunderstorms, thunderclaps, protection.)

Step 7: Synthesise and test the new information
In the following tutorial, the results of the self-study activities are reviewed and related back to the learning goals set in the previous tutorial. Normally, around half of the meeting is devoted to this activity. During this phase, you attempt to discover common ground between the separate elements presented in the analysis. *Synthesizing* (defined as the process of combining or putting together), means that tutorial group members try to establish a common link between the aspects that they have found in the literature. The input of information from various sources can be highly beneficial to this process. Of course, it is impossible to discuss everything that has been studied since the last meeting. The report, therefore, should perhaps focus on the following points:
- A short *summary* of the main points of the consulted literature;
- A *discussion* of the learning material that has not altogether been understood;
- A *review* of the discussion from the previous tutorial. This should centre on whether group members are now in a better position to recognise and understand the subject-related principles raised by the problem.

The report provides a good means of checking your own understanding and enhancing comprehension of the material. Explain in your own words what you have studied and make sure that the others are able to understand what you are saying. Use your notes to jog your memory, but do not read out word for word. When others are speaking, ask yourself whether you understand what they are saying and if you believe their standpoint to be accurate.

Assimilation of the material also implies that the tutorial has not simply restricted itself to addressing the learning goals, but has also managed to provide insight into the *interrelationship* of the answers and the *context* in which they fit.

For example, does the subject matter deal with constituents of a much wider area of study, and what is the relationship with the issues dealt with in the previous problems? With this in mind, the discussion leader (or someone else) can summarise the main points of the report again with the assistance, where necessary, of the tutor.

Box 16 provides an example of this process.

Box 16 *Example of step 7: Synthesising and testing new information. Fragments of the discussion on 'A warm summer's day'*

Chair:	Welcome. On the blackboard I've written the learning goals we formulated at last meeting. Shall we start off by discussing the various learning resources we've studied? (All group members bring out their references to their learning resources.) Okay, let's start. The first learning goal was the meaning of the word 'welkin'.
Sarah:	The Oxford dictionary describes it as an Old English word for heaven or the firmament. It's a literary word today, used to describe a sky filled with huge, dark clouds looming in the distance.
Chair:	Anybody else? (Looks around, nobody reacts). Okay. The second learning goal was on electricity. We wondered whether it occurs between or in clouds. And, how does the lightning process develop? Jane, will you be first?
Jane:	There is no difference in current in between clouds as such but there are differences in the whole area of the thunderstorm. How the process goes on isn't clear to me yet.
John:	Thunderstorms in our region mostly start after a few days of warm weather. Then you get changes in the atmosphere when, e.g. a cold area of low pressure moves close to a warm high pressure area. In the warm area, moist air rises. These vertical currents, called convection currents, cannot dissipate in the higher layers because of the flow of cold air. That warm convection current…
Peter:	(Interrupts). I don't get it. Cold air drops. In that case the cold air should be underneath the hot air.
John:	Well, no, I thought that… Um, you have to consider this on an enormous scale. Tremendous quantities of air are involved in the collisions in the higher layers of the atmosphere. That's why you can see thunderheads, cumulonimbus clouds, those clouds that look like an anvil. They can

stretch over ten to fifteen kilometres in the sky. When it rises, moist warm air cools down and the moisture changes in structure. It condenses. First it becomes water vapour, then rain drops, later on ice crystals. And during this process the charged particles change their charge.

Sarah: Yes, exactly! Depending on the size of the raindrops or ice crystals, they become either positively or negatively charged. The crystals of ice get ripped apart by the violent turbulence. The bigger crystals have a negative charge, the smaller ones positive. The bigger ice crystals fall, the splinters of ice are thrust upwards. After a while, more particles with a positive charge are in the higher layers, while the majority of particles with a negative charge are in the lower layers of the clouds. You have to realise, however, that there are local differences in those enormous banks of clouds. There could of course be positive charges in the lower layers as well as negative ones in the higher layers.

Eva: Oh, so does that difference in electrical charges actually cause lightning to flash between the sky and the earth?

Tutor: Wait a moment, not so fast. Can somebody explain how those bigger ice crystals get a negative charge, and the splinters of ice a positive one?

Eva: Don't know, exactly. I read in the literature that even experts don't understand that process exactly. They certainly don't agree about it.

Tutor: It's still important to try to understand this process. Does anybody else have information?

Tom: I know of several theories that leave lots of things unclear. The most current opinion is that ascending droplets of moisture freeze when they collide with the ice crystals already in the higher layers. The freezing begins on the outside of the droplet. During this process heat is released and gets admitted to the inner part of the droplet. Because the outer layer freezes before the inside does, this creates a difference in temperature and this starts up a small electric charge, the process called thermoelectricity during which the frozen outer part becomes positive, and the fluid inside becomes negative. As the process of freezing persists, the water expands and the raindrops burst apart into icy splinters charged positive and heavier super cooled fluid cores charged negative. As Sarah mentioned earlier, the light parts float on up on the upward current, while the heavier parts drop downwards. This explains the different charges in different parts of the clouds.

(Discussion continues)

Chair: Okay, I think everybody now understands the process of electricity formation in clouds. (Looks around.) Let's go on now and discuss lightning. Jane just said that the differences in charge are responsible for the fact that the lightning goes from sky to earth. Would you like to tell us more?

Jane: (Looks at the table in front of her, keeps quiet.)

Tom: It's putting it too simply to think that only positive charges are in the upper layers of clouds, and negative ones are only found in the layers below. In reality the positive and negative charges are everywhere, only more positive ones are in the upper layers than below, and vice versa. It's all relative. You have to imagine that in those areas with both positive and negative charges, the negative ones, the electrons, are very agile. The electrons accelerate in their electronic field and in this way they develop something called pre-discharges between the plusses and minuses.

John: Exactly! Small electric currents start up deep inside the cloud, creating tiny lightning flashes that are barely visible to our eyes. These pre-discharges look for routes offering less resistance. Gradually they develop conductive channels, the so-called step leaders. And when these usually very fanciful paths are ready, then the real lightning has a route to follow.

Tutor: Hang on a moment, John. Tom, you just told us something about accelerating electrons. How does this actually create electricity?

Tom: Perhaps I've got it all wrong. (Looks through his notes.) Um, yes, those accelerating electrons… they're moving very quickly in a small area of plusses and minuses. The movement becomes bigger and bigger, eventually so big that the electrons ionise the surrounding air molecules when they crash against each other. And that process makes new charges of plusses and minuses develop. All this dashing about and developing new plusses and minuses just goes on and on. So the ionisation process becomes huge, which means tremendous differences in current, especially in the lower layers of the clouds.

Sarah: Those ionising areas move about because of air turbulence. You have to imagine that all this happens very, very quickly, in microseconds. And at huge velocities. Gradually a path develops in the direction of earth.

Eva: That's weird. I read that lightning starts on earth and goes up to the clouds. I don't understand that.

John: Ah, I'll try to explain. In general the earth has a negative current with respect to the ionosphere. But the earth is also a good conductor of electricity. At the bottom of our cloud is an enormous field of negative current. This repels against the negative current in the bit of earth surface located precisely under our cloud. At this location the earth becomes positively charged. When there is sufficiently high difference in charge between earth and the lower layers of the clouds, a relatively small flash of lightning can leave the surface and go *up* to the clouds. Meanwhile the conduction paths in the clouds have been building up. The current travels down and along these paths with enormous heat and potential and contacts the earth.

Tom: I agree with that explanation. And, did you know, those strokes of lightning are necessary. Normally, current flows from earth to the ionosphere. You can say that the earth is gradually losing its current. Thunderbolts actually bring this current back down to earth. So there is an interchange between earth and the ionosphere. In our part of the world thunderstorms and thunderbolts don't happen that often, but in the tropics they occur really often.

Tutor: I see that on the board our scribe has made a fantastic drawing of this explanation. Will someone briefly summarise the process for us?

(Anne summarises. The discussion goes on for a while)

Chair: Our third learning goal was: is the thunderclap caused by an explosion or implosion?

Jane: The main electrical discharge is accompanied by very high temperatures and velocities. This means the surrounding air moves and expands. In other words, it's an explosion. We call the sound of this violent movement thunder. Light moves faster than sound. That's why you see lightning first and hear thunder later. If you start counting immediately after you see the lightning, you can calculate how far away the thunderstorm is from you. About three beats stand for one kilometre. As the path of a thunderbolt can be many kilometres long you can hear thunder way off in the distance. And of course, there are not only vertical lightning bolts but also horizontal ones. People call thunderclaps in a far distance rumbling.

(Discussion goes on)

Chair: Okay, let's start discussing the next learning goal: How can we protect ourselves from thunderstorms. First, what can we do when we are in an open area. Can you give us some information, Tom?

Tom: It's very dangerous to shelter under a tree. When lightning strikes a tree the current goes through the cambium, the wet living tissue between the bark and the heart of the tree, down to the ground. The heat creates steam which blows the bark off the tree. It can cause electrocution or severe burns, even cardiac arrest.

Sarah: There are four ways you could be hit by a thunderbolt: directly, by a side flash, step, or contact current. Out in the open the best protection is to look for a gully, crouch down in it and make yourself as small as possible.

Eva: I looked up that Faraday cage thing. Faraday discovered that electronic current comes together on the outside surface of hollow objects. A car is such a hollow object which is why you'd be safe sheltering inside a car.

Paul: But where does the current go?

Chair: Stop. Stop. We're jumping from topic to topic too quickly. Let's go back. Sarah, you told us about the four ways of being hit by a thunderbolt. Tell us more about that…

(Discussion goes on)

Creating a more detailed report can lead to the formulation of additional learning goals:

- Sometimes new questions are raised during the report;
- Sometimes it turns out that the problem was not defined clearly enough at first, making it impossible to achieve the expected results;
- Sometimes in the self-study phase, individuals generate questions that might be important for the whole group to consider.

Students can investigate new lines of study based on these additional learning goals and report on them in the next tutorial meeting. Vary the way in which you report back to the tutorial on the findings you have made from the literature studied. Encapsulate the concepts and interrelationships in the form of a diagram (see section 4.4), which can be used as a basis for the report.

From time to time the tutorial group will be confronted by problems for which no clear explanation seems to exist, even when the study material has been examined extensively and discussed in depth. Sometimes the tutor will be able to help, but this might not always be the case. The problems set down in the module book relate to a wide range of fields and the tutor may not have expertise in a specific area. At this point, the tutorial group may find it useful to call on the services of an *expert* who has a thorough knowledge of the subject in question. Once the tutorial has decided to consult an expert, students must perform two activities to benefit fully from the contribution of the expert concerned. Firstly, the group needs to find out who exactly can be consulted and, secondly, students need to carefully prepare a set of questions for the expert.

The tutorial group will be able to find the best authority to ask either by checking through the list of experts in the module book, going through a general list of lecturers, or through the tutor or module co-ordinator. Group members must decide on how they want to consult this expert. For example, they may wish to invite the expert to the next tutorial meeting or they can ask some group members to contact the person in question separately. It all depends on the nature of the problem for which the expert needs to be consulted. If it concerns a problem on which opinions are divided within the group or which group members consider essential for everyone to understand properly, it is better to ask the expert to attend the tutorial. If it concerns a secondary matter that needs clearing up but because of its nature, does not require the presence of everyone, the group can decide to send a few members as delegates. It is desirable to send more than one member to the expert to make sure that information doesn't get lost.

Of course, the expert in question may be unavailable because of other commitments. In some modules, contact with experts can be planned in advance by scheduling question and answer sessions. Agree beforehand on who should go to such a meeting to ask the questions.

If contact with the expert is to be productive, the group must think very carefully about how to phrase the questions. The expert must be able to form a clear picture of the background to the question. So explain the context of the problem in relation to the module and briefly describe to what extent the group has already studied the problem. Sometimes an expert will need time to prepare an answer to the questions. If the group decides to invite the expert to the tutorial meeting, it would be a good idea to give prior warning of your expectations. For example, arrange a mini-lecture, followed by a discussion or seminar in which the expert can help students to understand the problem by providing examples, asking questions or clarifying information.

2.5   Strategy problems

Strategy problems focus on the activities of a professional practitioner. For those pursuing medical training, this will mainly concern the role of a physician; for legal studies, a lawyer and for psychology, a psychologist. A strategy problem requires that you take on the role of a doctor, legal expert or psychologist. The aim of this type of problem is to teach you how to make rational judgements in your own professional domain on the basis of underlying processes, mechanisms or procedures (with which you have familiarised yourself by studying explanation problems). In strategy problems, the emphasis is on (1) the formulation of activities, procedures, or methods necessary for solving a particular problem, (2) the 'why' of these particular strategies, and (3) arguments for or against each activity. Boxes 17 and 18 give examples of strategy problems.

Box 17 *Example of a strategy problem in law*

> *Ito*
> You are acting as lawyer for Rachel Jones and Ito Gio. For the last sixth months, Rachel has been living with Ito Gio, a Bulgarian immigrant worker. Their future together looks gloomy ever since Ito was caught red-handed making a forcible entry, committing burglary and handling stolen goods. Ito has been sentenced to eight months in prison, minus his remand period, plus a probationary period of two years. However, now that Ito has been threatened with deportation as a result of the Minister of Justice withdrawing his residence permit, the situation has become even worse. At the end of her tether, Rachel says she will marry him if this is the only way to prevent his deportation.
> What actions should you take as their lawyer ?

Box 18 *Example of a strategy problem in psychology*

> 1. On a warm summer night a man and a woman return to their car after visiting a restaurant. In the moonlit parking lot they are suddenly confronted by two young men, one with a knife in his hand. They grab the woman without the man being able to do anything. 'Your money or we'll kill her,' whispers one

of the men. The threatened man hands over his wallet, he and the woman are thrown to the ground, and the young men disappear into the night.

2. A man hits his wife and shouts at her. He is drunk. He then rips off her clothes and tries to rape her. At the door of the bedroom, five-year old Kim watches.

Suppose that you are a psychologist. You are asked by the police to provide guidelines on how these eyewitnesses should be interrogated to obtain valid information. What would you recommend?

The question raised by the example illustrated in box 17 is the following: which actions could you undertake to help Rachel and Ito? What steps could be taken to delay or prevent Ito's deportation? It should be clear that the formulation of a strategy presupposes some degree of knowledge, e.g. in this case, knowledge of the law on expulsion and related procedures.

To work effectively on strategy problems, it is important to follow clear-cut procedures. Firstly, the group will have to decide what exactly is expected from them with regard to the problem at hand. Subsequently group members, using their prior knowledge, will have to formulate the steps they would take if they were in the position of the doctor, the lawyer or the psychologist. It is important for groups to justify their strategy. Why take a particular set of steps and why follow them in a particular order? What are the possible pros and cons of each step? During discussion, differences of opinion and some uncertainty will emerge as to which steps should be taken. These differences of opinion may give you cause to formulate specific learning goals. When the discussion is over, you will need to cross-check the chosen strategy with the strategies explained in reference books, etc. The focus should always be on the 'why' question. Why is a particular strategy the best for dealing with a particular problem? Why should the professional act in a particular way and not in another way? What is the scientific evidence supporting that particular strategy? These aspects can form part of the synthesis during the subsequent tutorial.

Of course, the group should first formulate the necessary steps based on existing knowledge, given that you have been confronted with the situation described in the problem. For example, if you need to formulate a number of questions, it is a useful exercise to ask yourself why each question might be important.

For some strategy problems, the tutor will have access to the necessary answers. If this is the case, the group can put a formulated strategy to the test straight away and, if necessary, make adjustments. However on each occasion the group must reach an agreement on what the next step is to be, followed by a response to that step. Don't try firing ten questions all at once, but decide at each point what the next question should be, and what information the answer will produce. Take stock of those aspects that are unclear, so that you are able to formulate learning goals. Here too it is essential to study external sources of information in order to gain a better understanding of reasoned professional methods.

2.6 Dilemma problems

As a professional you have to take a critical stance towards subjects. These subjects relate to the normative or social aspects of the profession for which you are being trained, i.e. matters in which personal values and opinions play a big part. The aim of dilemma problems is to prompt the student to look more critically at the various opinions that exist related to a specific subject. For example, there might be two different theories to explain a particular phenomenon. Students are then asked to evaluate the pros and cons of both of these theories. Dilemma problems will prepare you for your future professional life where you will be required to express and justify your opinions articulately. Examples of dilemma problems are presented in boxes 19 and 20.

Box 19 *Example of a dilemma problem in the health sciences*

Blood transfusion for a Jehovah's Witness child.
A child is admitted to the First Aid Ward of a hospital. She has been knocked down by a car and has lost a substantial amount of blood. A transfusion is the only way to save the child's life, in the judgment of the attending physician. However there is a problem. The parents are unlikely to give their consent because their religion forbids the transmission of another person's blood to their child's body: 'She is in God's hands.' If, despite this, transfusion takes place, the parents will reject the child.
What do you think the physician should do?

Box 20 *Example of a dilemma problem in psychology*

Differences of opinion

Statement 1a. Knowledge of biological processes is irrelevant for understanding psychological processes.

Statement 1b. Knowledge of the brain and of biological processes is essential for understanding psychological processes.

Statement 2a. The human psychological processes of behaviour, sensation, emotion, and cognitive functioning are so similar to the same psychological processes in higher animals that studying these processes in animals is useful.

Statement 2b. The human psychological processes of behaviour, sensation, emotion, and cognitive functioning are so dissimilar to the same psychological processes in higher animals that studying these processes in animals is useless.

Statement 3a. The brain produces behaviour like kidneys produce urine.

Statement 3b. Behaviour can never be reduced to biological processes.

A discussion surrounding a dilemma problem is sometimes seen as a battle to be won or lost. Individuals make their viewpoint known and try to convince others by using a stream of arguments, clever reasoning, guileful techniques and other debating skills. However, this is not the purpose. The intention is not to find a specific (i.e. an absolute) opinion. The point is that participants should become aware of their own opinions, the opinions of other group members as well as the professional norms and values on an issue. The aim is to become aware that many issues can be viewed from different angles.

This form of discussion is a creative process. You should be prepared to put forward your own ideas but, at the same time, also be prepared to modify your standpoint. To do this, you should listen carefully to what others have to say and try to understand what they mean.

To raise the quality of the discussion in the tutorial group when working on a dilemma problem, careful planning is essential. The following six steps can be used in the planning process:

1 Clarify any troublesome terms and concepts.
2 Define the problem.
3 Set down the different opinions and viewpoints.
4 Arrange these viewpoints into some order.
5 Discuss the main points in-depth.
6 Formulate conclusions (possible learning goals).

Steps 1 and 2 are intended to parallel the same steps as in the seven-step model for studying explanation problems, i.e. to clarify the core of the discussion and to elucidate points for subsequent work. To make good headway in the discussion, it is vital to formulate the problem definition coherently. This is, however, not always possible. Sometimes the problem is obvious, but in many situations the group needs to reach an agreement on exactly what the central issue of the discussion is. Apart from identifying the central topic of discussion, a decision also has to be made regarding the definition of the problem. It is important to involve all the members of the tutorial group in this decision-making process. In situations where the development of opinions is important, it is critical to have as many participants involved as possible. A good way of ensuring that everyone contributes is to ask everyone in turn what he or she considers to be the central issue.

Step 3 marks the actual start of the discussion. Initially, the group will take stock of the various opinions surrounding the discussion topic. Each group member will be expected to contribute. At this stage, you should be careful not to argue the various opinions too intensely. This step is characterised by an exploration of the different viewpoints. It is also important not to brush off any opinions. Make sure that all points of view are considered. The discussion leader has a key role to play here. Make a list of the different points of view on a board, so that they are clear to each of the group members. Once people's views have been registered in this way, it will be less (or no longer) necessary to keep returning to them again. Once a clear picture has emerged of the different viewpoints, ideas and opinions, step 4 can begin, i.e. putting the various points of view into some sort of order.

Non-relevant aspects can be filtered out and the key aspects juxtaposed. The purpose of categorising the different viewpoints in this way is to avoid an interminable discussion. It is a necessary pre-condition for step 5, the phase in which the plausibility of the different arguments is examined in depth. This can be done in a variety of ways, e.g. by getting proponents and opponents of a particular standpoint to present their arguments in turn. You might also want to split the tutorial into smaller groups of people with similar opinions and allow them to develop their arguments in greater detail before opening the discussion up to the whole group again.

The final step is important to prevent the discussion from dying a sudden death. Try to organise and summarise all that the group has learned. For some topics, there will be outstanding points of uncertainty, at least for some members of the group. If this is the case, additional learning goals can be set. Aim to meet these goals by making further enquiries, i.e. by studying the literature, consulting audio-visual resources or talking to experts in the field. In the example relating to blood transfusion in box 20, group members might want to consider the thoughts and writings of ethicists on this problem, and how specific actions might affect the legal rights and obligations of professionals working within health services. You might even think about inviting someone to speak who has regular first-hand experience of such occupational hazards.

2.7   Other types of problems

This chapter has dealt with a number of important types of problems and the approaches to study associated with them. You will soon find out, however, that the problems included in module books cannot always be pigeon-holed into the forms that we have described so far. It also means that the tutorial group will have to modify its approach from time to time.

Sometimes you will find that teachers or specific assignments in a module book ask you to apply newly acquired knowledge to problems that are more or less analogous to the original problem you discussed in the tutorial group.

In *assignments*, the study material, key points and the appropriate material are specified explicitly. Problems of this type usually begin with the words 'Please study the following ....', or some similar such phrasing. Boxes 21 and 22 offer examples.

Box 21 *Example of an assignment in economics*

Competition
Study Chapter 4 , Competitiveness and competitive position, in Daems & Douma, *Competition: analysis and strategy*, 2004.
Please note: this assignment is intended for individual study. The material studied will be applied during the following section of this module.

Box 22 *Example of an assignment in law*

Does the punishment really fit the crime?
Lawyers representing the 'Gang of Maastricht' are meeting to discuss whether
any benefit can be gained from lodging an appeal. In their opinion, the arguments
made in the judgement were somewhat weak. According to the judges, the penal-
ties imposed are all in keeping with the seriousness and nature of the offences
committed and take into consideration the personality of the accused. The remark-
able thing was that in the case of Sjo, the court went far beyond the demands of
the public prosecutor. In the sentencing of Sjra, the judgement contains no trace
of the defence of the punishment that was so explicitly called for ('no treatment,
but community service').
Study J. de Hullu, Grounds for punishment. In G. Knigge (ed.). *Case studies in
the law of criminal procedure*. (See electronic reader). Groningen, 1995.

An assignment invites the user to engage in individual study activities, either at
home or in the library. The aim is to enable the student to acquire knowledge
about the subject matter. Often an assignment will be used as a platform for
studying new problems that otherwise you wouldn't have been able to understand
without first having studied the literature.

In contrast to other forms of problems, the tutorial group is not expected to enter
into discussions before the study material has been studied. However, it is important to agree in the tutorial group beforehand on the way in which reports will be
made in the next tutorial.

In studying your assignments, we encourage you to ask yourself how much you
already know about the subject in question. One useful way to do this is to draw
up a diagram of the most important items in the study material. Chapter 4 of this
book offers tips on how to do this.

For carrying out assignments, work according to the following four steps:
1   Read the assignment carefully and figure out what is expected.
2   Agree on how the report should be presented in the next tutorial (e.g. compar-
    ing diagrams or discussing unclear aspects of the literature studied).
3   Self-study.
4   Report to the tutorial group in the agreed way.

Application problems are devised to provide the student with an opportunity to
put acquired knowledge into practice. Types of application problems include
practical assignments, numerical exercises and problem-solving activities. Usually, the application contains an element of combining different aspects of knowledge or of deriving new facts from available information. In many disciplines it
is very important to apply specific principles and, as such, application problems
are very useful in helping to achieve this.

Application problems can also occur in a module as a means of evaluation. Group members can check whether they have a proper understanding of the material studied and whether they are able to apply it in practical situations. Box 23 gives an example of an application problem.

Box 23 *Example of an explanation problem in law*

It never rains, but it pours
Explanatory note: below are a number of case studies. When solving the case studies, the aim is to re-examine the subject matter dealt with in the preceding problems.
A.
Tracy, aged 34, has been placed under a supervision order. She lives on her own because she is able to look after herself properly. One day, Tracey gives notice that she wishes to terminate the tenancy agreement on her apartment. The housing association promises the apartment to someone else who has been on the housing waiting list for three years.
B.
Robert is astonished to find an LCD TV priced at 750 euro in the window of a local hi-fi shop. Elsewhere in town the LCD TVs are 250 euro more expensive. He goes into the shop to buy the TV only to find out from the shop owner that he has made a mistake with the price tag and that it in fact costs 950 Euro.

Sometimes you will find *a mix of the types of problems* that have been described earlier. These types of problems are offered to help you understand that in your professional life, understanding the underlying mechanisms, processes or structures goes hand in hand with solving problems. Explanation problems and strategy problems are interwoven. Learning to act as a professional expert means that you are able to understand scientific theories and to solve problems in a practical way. Boxes 24 and 25 offer examples.

Box 24 *Example of a combination of an explanation and a strategy problem in psychology*

Little monsters
Coming home from work tired and in need of a hot bath, Anita, an account manager, discovers two spiders in her tub. She shrinks back, screams, and runs away. Her heart is pounding and a cold sweat comes over her. A neighbour saves her from distress by catching the little monsters by hand and putting them outside. Anita's neighbour often has to help her to get rid of spiders. While drinking a coffee together one day, she suggests that it may be wise for Anita to seek help and get treatment for arachnophobia.
Although Anita is initially hesitant, she decides to get some help and is now sitting in your office telling you about her irrational fear of spiders.

Box 25 *Example of a problem in medicine to be explained at more than one level*

> *A Guinea worm infection*
> In the spring of 1979, a group of medical students on a community health posting discovered an epidemic of Guinea worm in Dekala, an isolated village in the Borghu, Nigeria. More than ninety percent of the inhabitants showed signs of the worm under their skin, in particular in the arms and legs. Many of them had open wounds at the places where the worms were emerging. Some were in very poor condition, experiencing fever and weakness.
> For water, the village relied on a dirty hole in the ground, the only source of drinking water during the dry season. There were no other facilities for obtaining drinking water. Among the few cases not affected by the disease were children under two years of age and the Sariki's family. (The Sariki is the leader of the village.) In response to a health education broadcast received on a transistor radio, he had been boiling drinking water for himself and for his family.

Other types of problems are also possible. For instance, the authors of a module might ask you to put together a particular product as the ultimate goal of the problem, such as a statement or an organisational diagram. Sometimes a group might be expected to present these results before a panel of experts. Additionally, students might also be required to undertake a number of practical activities outside the group as part of a problem, such as data collection exercises and the electronic analysis of results or a laboratory test.

In other courses, the focus is on the conception of new, creative solutions for the problems put forward. Examples of this can be found within the fields of architecture and industrial design. A tutorial will have to adopt a working method that suits the purpose of the problem set. When making a problem analysis for design specifications, the emphasis will be centred on discussions regarding the pre-conditions surrounding the design (e.g. what are the functional requirements? What materials need to be used? What environmental considerations are there?).
In courses where problem-based learning has a prominent role, teachers are expected to be imaginative and deal with the subject matter in an active and appealing manner. By using the procedures that have been outlined in this chapter, you will undoubtedly be better able to develop a creative approach to dealing with these different forms and combinations.

It would be go beyond the bounds of this book to describe extensively the way in which the tutorial should tackle all these different forms or combinations. Some other methods that could be used in explaining or solving theoretical or practical professional problems are the mind-mapping technique, the topical question list, the fishbone diagram, and SWOT analysis.[10] For example, the fishbone or

10 The list of references at the end of the book contains several sources of more information on these methods.

'Ishihawa' diagram (named after its inventor) allows a tutorial group to map out all the factors that affect the problem or a desired outcome. Problem definition describes a cause and effect relationship. The diagram in a completed form resembles the skeleton of a fish. SWOT analysis stands for Strengths, Weaknesses, Opportunities and Threats. SWOT analysis has become a popular tool used to analyse internal and environmental forces promoting or hindering change in a team or an organisation.

2.8 Variations in problem-based learning

Throughout the previous sections, you have been introduced to problem-based learning in its traditional format. You have learned how to work in this kind of learning environment. Unfortunately our recommendations are sometimes interpreted as set instructions that must be followed to the letter. However we consider them rather as tools that promote active learning both inside and outside of the tutorial group. When students have gained more experience in handling a variety of problems, it can be refreshing to try different problem-solving approaches. Variations in the way problems are presented can also inspire students to seek out other ways of tackling a problem.

Some of these variations will be discussed in this section, including variations in problem analysis, in the division of work among group members and in reporting. We conclude with a section on educational approaches related to PBL.

2.8.1 Variations in problem analysis

Once you have applied the seven-step model twice a week for a semester you may get bored doing the same thing over and over again. This may lead to superficial discussions and cutting corners, formulating learning goals without really exploring what the group already knows about the problem. Here are a few suggestions for handling problem analysis differently.

Using 'Post-it' notes
This is an alternative to using the brainstorming technique introduced earlier.
- Each group member writes initial ideas on a self-adhesive 'Post-it' note, one idea per note.
- All notes are stuck on a board and group members can add written comments.
- Then the group tries to cluster ideas by putting related ideas together.
- After that the group sits down and discusses the clustered ideas.

Subgroups making a problem analysis from a particular viewpoint
In many fields there are clear distinctions between professional points of view and professional roles. For example, between marketing and finance in business studies; between treatment and prevention in health sciences.

Divide the group into subgroups, each of which will then analyse the problem from a different professional perspective. Each subgroup then makes a short presentation, and the whole group will discuss the outcomes of the two analyses.

Nominal group technique
In this approach, interaction between group members is minimal in the initial problem analysis.

- Each group member makes an individual problem analysis on paper without consulting other group members.
- Each group member presents an analysis, to be summarised on the blackboard by a scribe and clustered if possible. There is no discussion.
- All suggestions are clarified by their originators.
- Each group member then revises his/her initial analysis based on what was presented by other group members.
- The most popular explanations or solutions are then discussed by the group.

Problem analysis in an electronic learning environment: The virtual tutorial
This is a variation on the approach just described. An important difference is that students work on their first analysis at home, then post it on the group space in an electronic learning environment, where they can also make comments and ask questions relating to the contributions of other group members. When the group then meets they can develop possible explanations and solutions, and formulate learning goals.

Problem analysis using decision-making software
In the analysis of complex policy and technological problems, professionals often make use of software which allows multi-phased discussion and decision-making. Such working environments can also be utilised in a PBL course. All group members in the 'decision room' are connected online to each other and to a moderator. The moderator asks for initial ideas and comments. At regular intervals the support or interest for ideas is tested by ranking them using the computer work station. The software then provides a group ranking. Without a direct person-to-person discussion, complex problems can be broken down via analysis into components for further exploration.

2.8.2   Variations in dividing the work among group members
In previous sections we assumed that all students in a tutorial group are working on the same learning goals in preparation for the next tutorial. Here too, variations are possible.

- A problem may be too complex to study completely within the time available. Dividing the work within the group provides a way to solve a problem in less time. PBL then changes into a micro-project, where students specialise in certain parts of the problem. They have to rely on the summaries of other students to understand the other components of the problem.
- Previously we mentioned the use of subgroups during initial problem analysis. Along the same lines, subgroups can also study a problem from a particular point of view or perspective, and report their findings in the next tutorial.

2.8.3 Variations in reporting

Elsewhere in this book we explained that during reporting, each student summarises the most important findings from the literature he/she has studied.

For more experienced students here are some suggestions for different ways of reporting.

- *'What I didn't understand…'* Rather than reporting findings, each group member formulates an issue which is not clear to him/her to the other group members, who then try to answer based on what they discovered during their own research.
- *Critical peer review.* Professionals are often required to present their findings to a critical audience of peers. As preparation for this situation, you can ask one student to give a complete presentation of the problem, followed by critical questions by other members of the group who have also studied the problem.

2.9   Educational approaches related to problem-based learning (PBL)

PBL is not a single prescribed educational method, but has grown out of quite diverse practices developed in various parts of the world, in a variety of disciplines and at various school levels. The common denominator among the various approaches is the emphasis on active learning using a problem as the stimulus and starting point for the learning process. Local circumstances and practices influence aspects such as the availability of resources for self study, group size, frequency and duration of tutorials during the week, the number of problems presented in a course, levels of teacher control over learning, and many others. Differences in cultural expectations and differences in national educational systems also influence the way PBL is used in programs. It would take too long to give examples of all of these different practices. It is also difficult to predict the effect of these different formats on learning outcomes. Some may yield good results, whereas others will not achieve the results discussed earlier.

In this final section we would briefly like to mention some educational approaches that can be considered to be related to PBL: case-based learning and project-based learning.

Case-based learning existed even before PBL was developed. In fact, it was one of the methods which inspired others to develop PBL. Case-based learning is popular in fields such as law and business studies. The main fact that distinguishes it from PBL is that a case is presented after students have received the information to solve the problem in lectures and required readings. Sometimes students are encouraged to search for extra information to help them understand the problem. The emphasis is on applying knowledge and skills to solve a problem. Students work individually or in small teams to analyse the case and to prepare a presentation of their solution to a larger group, including a teacher who is an expert on the case at hand.

Project-based learning also existed before PBL. Like PBL, it has gained more supporters over the last few decades. Projects are generally larger in size than the problems used in PBL. In small teams, students are encouraged to divide the work among themselves and assemble the various pieces into a final result. Project themes are generally linked to real-life problems and participation of professionals facing those problems is quite common and provides additional motivation for students in trying to find a fitting solution.

Project-based learning is used widely in engineering courses, but is also applied as a follow-up to PBL in a variety of other fields, such as health policy studies and business education.

Projects may last a semester and may fill up 20-50% of the total course load during that time. The team size is variable, but in most courses the size is four to eight persons. Each team has to develop a project plan showing the deadlines for the various stages of the project. The team works without a teacher present and reports back during a larger meeting in which all project teams participate. Teachers generally have a supervisory function and can be called in for help. Usually two products have to be developed: a final report showing the result of the project which may contain a model or prototype; and a report on the working process of the project team.

In summary: The previous sections suggested the importance of choosing a working method which best suits the set problem. Problem-based learning represents a practical approach to learning, which means that work in a tutorial group should remain active and educational. Perhaps the guidelines given in this chapter will be interpreted by some as representing hard and fast rules from which no deviation is possible. However, we must emphasise that the procedures described here are simply tools to help you learn to work effectively with problems. When you have gained more experience in working with problems, you will be surprised at the novel ways in which you will be able to tackle a problem. Of course, do not simply choose a method where learning goals are formulated on the basis of a problem simply to save time. The most important thing is to continue tackling problems in an active fashion and applying the knowledge you have acquired to analyse the problem effectively. If the group wishes to adopt a different working method, the way in which the problem is to be tackled needs to be made clear to everybody.

3 Collaborative learning in the tutorial group

3.1 Introduction

Being able to work with others is a required skill today in most professions. The size and complexity of problems with which organisations and society are confronted require intradisciplinary as well as interdisciplinary teamwork. Being an expert in your field is not enough.

In order to function well in a team you must also have good social and communication skills. For example, you should be able to listen actively to others, have the potential to chair a team meeting, know how you can deal adequately with colleagues who are not functioning as well as be able to evaluate the progress made by a group and give colleagues adequate feedback. A tutorial group is a suitable place to acquire these skills.

3.2 What is a tutorial group?

In the psychological literature a group is defined as a collection of people who are working on a common purpose and who mutually influence each other by communicating directly with each other. We speak about a tutorial group when the purpose is to learn something, and when that learning takes place within the framework of a course of study. The discussion in a tutorial group aims to increase your knowledge and insight in a certain field of study and to develop informed opinions about academic, professional or societal questions. The tutorial group has a central role in problem-based learning. Because the mutual exchange of knowledge and ideas is important a tutorial group can only consist of a limited number of participants. Where groups consist of more than ten persons the chances for each member of the group to play an active part quickly become restricted.

3.3 The importance of learning in small groups

There are a number of reasons why learning in small groups is beneficial. First of all, the tutorial group provides the most favourable environment for *learning how to analyse problems*. Although nobody can say with any certainty how individuals solve problems, we do know that the exercise of analysing a specific problem is a method by which associated problems can be solved more efficiently and effectively. Important skills, which are acquired in the process, are:

- learning to dissect the problem into smaller or subordinate problems;
- learning to formulate ideas which enable the problem to be understood more easily;
- activating knowledge that has already been acquired, and
- adopting a critical attitude to the methods used.

An important part of acquiring these skills is the ability to ask questions. A tutorial offers you the opportunity not only to ask questions yourself, it also gives you the chance to learn from the questions posed by others.

Working in a tutorial group can also have a positive effect on a student's *motivation to learn*. This can happen in a variety of ways. A seemingly dull subject can suddenly take on a compelling new dimension when someone else talks about it, whilst a problem that had previously never occurred to you might prove thought provoking when it is thrashed out in the tutorial group. When you realise that your contributions are appreciated, you might be inspired to take your studies further than you would have otherwise. The notion that you are not working alone, but sharing the responsibilities with others might help you through a period of poor self-motivation during your course of study.

A tutorial group also enables you to compare your participation with that of your fellow students. This informal feedback on the quality and quantity on study is often viewed more favourably by students than more formal methods such as tests and exams.

An important argument in favour of working in tutorial groups is its focus on *communication skills*. In a tutorial, you are expected to ask questions, say something about an article or book that you've read or explain a complex item of study material. The tutorial provides you with the ideal platform to practice these skills on a regular and consistent basis. The tutorial is also an excellent setting in which to *learn to work with other people*. The tutorial group setting can also enable you to develop a number of other skills, such as delegating tasks and co-operating effectively with other students to fulfil shared objectives.

Finally, working in a tutorial group gives you the opportunity to learn something about the way *you and others function within a group*. The tutorial enables you to find out how others react to your contributions and how you yourself react to the contributions of others. Communal discussions about the progress of the group and the issues that arise will give you a better insight into this and provide an opportunity to improve your skills.

Collectively, these skills are likely to be important to you in your working-life. In the work environment, communication and collaborative skills rehearsed in the tutorial group will have to be converted into practice.

3.4   Collaborative learning in a tutorial group

The primary aim of a tutorial group is to achieve a better understanding of the subject matter offered to the students through the use of problems. Students must independently as well as in the group carry out a variety of learning activities. An overview of the various activities that contribute to learning information is given in box 26.[11]

Box 26 *Catergories of important learning activities for a tutorial group*

- *Structuring*: putting separate pieces of information together into an organised whole, attempting to structure the learning material and integrating the newly acquired knowledge with the knowledge that the student already possesses. Examples of this learning activity are: summarising parts of the discussion; displaying the core concepts from an article and the relationships between these in a clear plan (concept map); trying to discover the common theme in a theory or between different theories.
- *Relating*: searching for associations between different parts of the subject matter, between the parts and the whole, the principles of the subject matter and between new information and the own pre-knowledge. Examples of this learning activity are: showing the similarities and differences between theories; trying to discover the common features between one problem in the course book and a different one or between the sub-themes in a course book.
- *Making concrete*: trying to formulate actual propositions from abstract infor-mation, derived from phemonena that are already known. Examples of this learning activity are: thinking of examples and metaphors; relating information from learning materials to personal experiences; relating subjects to events in daily life.
- *Selecting*: distinguishing between principle and secondary matters, reducing large amounts of information to the most important parts. Examples of this learn-ing activity are: identifying core concepts; treating some subjects thoroughly and others more superficially; paying particular attention to certain types of information such as definitions or the main principles or practical applications.
- *Applying*: practising using the content of the subject matter. Examples of this learning activity are: applying new knowledge to the problem at hand or an analogous one; using the content of the teaching material to interpret experi-ences and events from the actual subject area; trying to explain new problems from the course book using what has been learned; coupling new information to actual professional developments and events.
- *Critically evaluating*: not just accepting everything that is written or said. Examples of this learning activity are: drawing one's own conclusions on the basis of facts and arguments; comparing the conclusions and visions of others against objective details; testing the logic of arguments; putting the opinions of experts into perspective and forming a personal opinion about the correctness of the information presented.

11 Vermunt, J.D. (1992). Ibid

- *Diagnosing*: identifying gaps in one's own knowledge and skills and in the command of the study material, investigating possible causes of problems and successes and of not (or not soon enough) discussing the subject matter. Examples of this learning activity are: finding out why a problem cannot be solved.
- *Reflecting*: thinking about all that has taken place during the discussions in the tutorial group and about the learning process, the instruction (quality of problems, the input and method used by the tutor), how the fellow students have worked together. Examples of this learning activity are: reflecting about the method followed; thinking about what learning activities were missing and should be tried out next time, assessing how the cooperation among the members of the group can be optimised.

A great deal of these learning activities takes place in a tutorial group. Group members suggest how to analyse a problem from a specific perspective, ideas are summarised and ordered, opinions are criticised and decisions taken. In the next section we give attention to some elementary characteristics of communication in tutorial group meetings. These characteristics are important for improving the functioning of the tutorial group.

3.5   Some elementary characteristics of communication

Discussion is an integral part of the tutorial group. Group members come forward with suggestions, ideas are raised and decisions taken. Either intentionally or unintentionally, a great deal of information is provided in the expectation that fellow participants will be stimulated, informed and changed by it. Much of this information, however, is received in restricted or distorted fashion. Not all the information exchanged in a tutorial is provided verbally. This section focuses on a number of elementary characteristics of communication which occur in any tutorial group and which can be of importance to observing and improving group function.

In addition to the transfer of information, communication may also have the aim of influencing others and can be distorted by emotions. People use all sorts of methods to communicate; besides speech this might include posture, hand gestures, tone of voice and facial expression. Often, the interpretation you give to someone's words (their *verbal communication*) only becomes clear when you have assimilated all the other forms of expression they use (their *non-verbal communication*). Though many students consider work in a tutorial as solely 'business-like' and 'task-related' in fact there are many other processes involved. Inevitably, co-operation creates a *social* situation in which certain expectations and feelings of participants play a role. Group members are always involved personally with the situation and will therefore experience emotions ranging from excitement and pleasure to worry, boredom or even anger. A tutorial group is therefore much more than a mere discussion of problems offered in a course book. The way in which group members interact also needs to be structured. Communication in a tutorial group involves two aspects:

1   Discussing the problems: The contributions made by the members of the group can be referred to as *task-related communication*. Task-related contributions are instrumental to being able to analyse and understand a specific problem. Such contributions may include suggesting solutions, presenting facts and figures, expressing an opinion, clarifying someone else's argument and summarising the discussion. Task-related contributions are focussed primarily on achieving group objectives.

2   Structuring the way in which group members interact: The contributions can be termed *group-related communication*. Clearly this is not just a one-off event that takes place at the start of the tutorial group. Anything agreed on at the beginning of the tutorial can be reconfirmed, modified or reformulated, directly or indirectly, and on a regular basis during the tutorial. Examples of group-related communication include allowing group members to make their contribution, encouraging individuals to elaborate on their views, describing the response of group members to certain proposals and questioning someone's level of participation. Group-related contributions regulate the relationships between group members and determine the influence each member of the group is able to exert.

The differences outlined above seem to suggest that *task-related* and *group-related* contributions can easily be differentiated, but that is not usually the case. A specific remark may contain a task-related and a group-related element at the same time. For example, if a group member says, 'I have every confidence that this theory is an important tool for improving our understanding of the problem', the contribution, on the one hand, is task-related since the person is offering an opinion on the choice that the group has to make. On the other hand, the tone of voice used and body language can make it clear that this student wants to exert an influence on the choice of priorities that the group will have to take in tackling the problem. This implies that the intentions of group members are often twofold, that is, they hope to influence both the task and the group function. Group-related communication is often more subtle especially if more controversial things need to be said. A group member is unlikely to say something like 'As long as I get my way when it comes to choosing the learning objectives' or 'I see your remarks as a personal attack and I aim to get even with you'. It is much more likely that a group member will try to express an opinion to fellow group members in a roundabout way, perhaps by being facetious, ironic or sarcastic. Box 27 offers an overview of important task-related and group-related behaviours that either fosters or hinders the ability of a tutorial group to work effectively and efficiently.[12]

12 Benne, K., & Sheats, P. (1948). Ibid

Box 27 *An overview of task-related and group-related behaviours that promote or hinder collaboration*

Behaviour that promotes progression in understanding subject-matter content within a tutorial group (task level):
- *Taking initiative:* e.g. putting forward new ideas; proposing solutions; making suggestions; redefining the problem; making suggestions for evaluation; clearing up confusion; motivating group members to continue.
- *Giving information:* e.g. giving facts or explanations; relating own experiences to the problems in the course book; showing the relationships between different ideas or proposals; giving examples and defining terms; showing similarities and differences; arranging the information in ordered form.
- *Asking for information:* e.g. questions to clarify relationships; questions for further information or facts; questions for examples; questions to coordinate ideas or proposals; questioning whether a particular theory can be applied to the problem.
- *Giving an opinion:* e.g. stating an opinion or conviction about earlier proposals; giving a critical evaluation of the opinions of an author; drawing conclusions on the basis of facts and arguments.
- *Asking for an opinion*: e.g. encouraging the members of the group to say what they think; looking for clarification of ideas; questioning whether the vision of the members of the group is in agreement with the facts.
- *Summarising*: e.g. ordering a part of the discussion; combining similar ideas or proposals; reformulating the suggestions made at the end of a group discussion; offering a conclusion or proposal for a learning objective to the group.

Behaviour that promotes collaboration within a tutorial group (group-related level):
- *Encouraging:* e.g. showing interest in other people's ideas; being prepared to answer others; showing appreciation for others and their ideas; openly agreeing with and accepting contributions from others.
- *Being a 'door-opener' or 'preparing the way':* e.g. stimulating others to have their say.
- *Formulating rules and procedures*: e.g. formulating group norms and rules that can be used for improving and maintaining the quality of the discussion with regard to content and cooperation.
- *Following:* e.g. going along with group decisions; listening actively; thoughtful acceptance of other people's ideas.
- *Expressing the group feeling:* e.g. describing the reactions of the group members to ideas or proposals; clarifying someone's opinion.

Behaviour that promotes both progress in understanding subject-matter content and collaboration within a tutorial group (task and group-related level):

- *Evaluating*: e.g. comparing what the group has achieved regarding the aims of the group; checking group decisions against the agreed procedures and rules; investigating how the cooperation is developing.
- *Diagnosing*: e.g. identifying sources of difficulty during the evaluation; analysing what is blocking the progress of the group.
- *Acting as an arbitrator*: e.g. reconciling different opinions with each other.
- *Reducing tension*: e.g. calming people down; making a joke at the right time; placing a tense situation in a broader context.

Behaviour that causes hindrance at task and group-related level:

- *Rivalry*: e.g. competing with others for the most productive or best ideas; trying to catch somebody out; going one better; scoring points; wanting to have the most to say; trying to butter up to the tutor.
- *Pursuing hobby horses*: e.g. only making or supporting those proposals that are concerned with the own opinions or philosophies.
- *Acting the fool*: e.g. continually making jokes; copying someone else; continually interrupting the group with misplaced jokes.
- *Attracting attention:* e.g. by talking too loud or too much; by putting forward extreme ideas or showing unusual behaviour.
- *Demonstrative withdrawal:* e.g. displaying uninterested behaviour; sitting whispering with others about a totally different subject; continually straying off the subject; restricting behaviour to formalities; daydreaming.
- *Blocking:* e.g. interrupting the progress of the group by concentrating on side issues; persistently continuing to argue about one point; rejecting the ideas of others without being prepared to think about them first.
- *Exaggerating:* e.g. group members who carry out certain activities to promote the progress of the group at any time whether appropriate or not, such as summarising, asking further questions, clarifying, coordinating, encouraging or expressing the feeling of the group.

The behaviour of others can also be strongly influenced by non-verbal communication. For example, if someone fixedly stares at the ceiling whilst another member of the group is explaining what they have studied during the previous week, it is likely to have an effect on the behaviour of the speaker. The speaker will probably interpret these actions as indifference and, as a result, may start to feel uneasy and put forward a less persuasive argument. However, this interpretation might be completely wrong – perhaps the listener is able to concentrate more easily when gazing in the distance and the speaker is unaware of this habit.

Box 28 lists a number of (mainly) non-verbal gestures. Try to examine the possible reasoning behind these gestures and the potential influence they might have on the other group members.

Box 28 *Gestures made in a group that may have an effect on the attitudes of others*

- leaning backwards and staring at the ceiling
- yawning continuously
- smiling
- tapping a pencil on the table
- reading your notes
- slowly shaking your head
- staring out of the window
- shrugging your shoulders
- nodding, um-ing and ah-ing
- sighing deeply
- raising your voice

If you've taken the time to do this exercise, you'll have noticed that it's often no easier to say with any certainty what the reason is for a particular gesture than to indicate what its effect is on others. The conclusion is to be cautious when interpreting non-verbal signals. After all, individuals express their feelings and desires in widely differing and sometimes contradictory fashions. Behaviour is often ambiguous in relation to the motives that precede it, but usually clear in the effects that it evokes in others.

3.6   Informal roles played out in the tutorial group

Each member of the tutorial group is charged with successfully clarifying and solving problems through task-related work and productive collaboration. The way in which this is carried out will vary from person to person. This is because group members differ from each other in a wide number of aspects. Here are just some:
- Personality
- Prior knowledge and education
- Age
- Experience and skills in working in groups
- Motivation to work in a tutorial group and to the task.
- Values and norms of the homeland.

We have already spoken about the possible consequences of some forms of communication within a group. We are, however, also confronted with *behavioural patterns*. If group members consistently show a specific behavioural pattern, it can be said that they are fulfilling an *informal role* in the tutorial.
These types of behavioural patterns can have a decisive effect on how the group performs. To illustrate this point, we will describe a number of behavioural patterns that may manifest themselves within a group. The descriptions should not be seen as permanent features as an individual is able to fulfil different roles at

different times and in different contexts. The choice of role is not only related to personal motives and characteristics, but also to other factors such as the topic being discussed and the roles being performed by the other group members.

Structuralists

These people's biggest concern is that other members of the group should contribute effectively. Without being asked, they assume the role of a spokesperson. If a state of confusion arises within the group, structuralists will manage to channel the contributions in such a way that discussions are able to proceed in an orderly fashion and will also suggest ways in which problems can be tackled.

Pacifiers

Pacifiers are great advocates of good personal relationships between group members. The aim of these people is to encourage a good working atmosphere and they will step in to play the role of mediator when rivalries occur in the group or there are personal confrontations between members of the group.

Windbags

Windbags have an opinion on everything and are always eager to express it even if no one else is interested. These people are not really interested in what other people say, but will butt in with their own remarks whenever someone else pauses to draw breath. Windbags are not so much conspicuous because of their views, but because of their irrepressible contributions.

Jokers

Jokers always have a joke up their sleeve to jolly the group along. In tense moments this may diffuse a difficult situation. However, because they persist in telling jokes in a serious discussion, this approach can also block progress and interfere with group function.

Snipers

These people see it as their duty to shoot down the contributions of others. They disagree with most of what is said and are at pains to make this obvious. They ask questions for which they already know the answer and are satisfied when the person questioned cannot give an answer. They also use non-verbal means of communication like shaking their head or adopting an indifferent posture.

Probers

Probers believe that the tutorial group is too easily inclined to skip certain issues. They believe that a subject should be looked at from every single angle. Sometimes they will need a whole month's intensive study before a specific task can be successfully concluded. This may get in the way of group progress. Conversely, they cram their heads with facts and have a thorough knowledge of the issues, so that whenever there's a problem relating to detail, the group can turn to them for advice and this may assist with group progress.

Whingers

These students always give the impression that the issues have not been tackled or analysed properly. When the rest of the group agrees, you can expect these people to make some whining remark about a minor inaccuracy. One moment they will be complaining about the task, the next about someone else's attitude. These people delay the group function in a largely unnecessary way.

The danger of these informal roles is that other group members will begin to anticipate the behaviour and start to react in such a way that any negative qualities become accentuated. This can lead to misunderstandings and inflexibility, which is not conducive to a good working atmosphere. For a tutorial group to function well, it is important to be aware of your own behavioural patterns and actively try to function constructively within the group. In doing so, you should take note of how others perceive you and whether there is a mismatch between your intention and the actual consequences of your style in the group. Chapter 5 will deal with this in more detail.

In addition to the informal roles played out within the group, there are also *formal roles*. The function of these is to encourage an efficient and effective way of working in the tutorial group.

3.7   Formal roles played out in the tutorial group

Formal roles are assigned on the basis of a member's formal position. Next, we will focus our attention on the respective positional roles in a tutorial group: the discussion leader, the scribe and the tutor.

3.7.1 The discussion leader

During tutorials, one student will be assigned the job of discussion leader or chair whose task it is to ensure that the discussion is conducted along structured lines. Commonly this role is rotated so that each student acts as chair once or twice during a module.

The discussion leader fulfils two types of functions within the tutorial:

1 *Task-related* functions: These activities carried out by the discussion leader are aimed at the content of and the approach to the problems set out in the module book.
2 *Group-related* functions: These actions will enhance the working atmosphere in the tutorial group.

The most important duty of a discussion leader is to ensure that the group makes progress in working towards its tasks. They will draw up the agenda, check on whether all the agreed aspects have been fulfilled, briefly introduce the subject to be dealt with and keep an eye on the time. The chair will give each group member an opportunity to make their contribution to the discussion by allowing them time to speak. They will provide structure by means of summarising progress regularly. They will also ensure that the subject to be dealt with is discussed and will bring the discussions to a close when the group members stray away from the subject.

An effective discussion leader will be interested primarily in the way the group goes to work on the problem. For preference, a discussion leader should not interfere with the content of the contributions. Experience shows that interfering with content leads to the responsibilities as discussion leader being neglected. Chapter 6 will discuss the responsibilities of the discussion leader in greater detail.

3.7.2 The scribe

During a tutorial, all the group members make a note of what has been discussed and decided, e.g., the learning objectives. Without these notes it would be difficult to know exactly what study activities to carry out between meetings. Nevertheless, the tutorial group needs a scribe to function effectively. When a problem is discussed, it is useful to record related information and make it available to the rest of the group. Important aspects of the discussion should be written up on the board, e.g., an overview of the various ideas brought forwards, a summary of solutions to a problem, a flow chart, an organisational diagram or a list of learning objectives that have been set. The scribe must ensure that remarks do not get lost in discussions and that a framework is constructed within which the group can work effectively towards solving a problem. In some courses, students are expected to produce the minutes of tutorial activity with a secretary preparing a report. Practice has shown that it is useful to have the scribe assume the role of the discussion leader in the subsequent meeting, since they will have a written record of all the important items agreed on at the previous meeting. The scribe's role will be dealt with in greater detail in Chapter 5.

3.7.3 The tutor

The tutorial group not only consists of students, a teacher is also present. Following the terminology of the founders of PBL at McMaster University, the teacher guiding a tutorial group is called a tutor. In some places the term 'facilitator' is used.

It is the responsibility of the tutor to stimulate the learning process amongst students and encourage collaboration. The tutor does not achieve this by lecturing, but by observing activities, posing questions and advising on the way in which students might be able to tackle the issues dealt with in the tutorial group to better effect.

To *stimulate the learning process* the tutor may encourage students to examine the study material in greater depth from time to time. This can be done in a variety of ways, e.g. by posing questions which activate a deeper and more channelled thought process, by illustrating the questions most applicable to a particular problem and the sequence and manner in which they can best be dealt with. The tutor may also provide case studies, draw comparisons with similar types of situations and direct students to specific literature.

To enhance the learning process of the group members, the tutor must try to gain an insight into the students' way of thinking. The tutor should stimulate students to ask the questions in much the same way as an expert would do in relation to the issue concerned. It can be difficult when students are confronted with fresh issues from a particular field of study for the first time. The tutor can help by pointing out misconceptions, faulty arguments or hypotheses and making suggestions as to how the student might acquire and process this new information. From time to time in the tutorial group there will be situations where a brief explanation of a particular subject is required because the students have got themselves bogged down in the material. A tutor with sufficient knowledge of the subject matter will be able to provide the necessary information. In general, however, the tutor will keep these explanations to a minimum and continue to encourage the students to gain a better understanding of the study material independently. The learning process is also stimulated by asking the group to examine exactly what they have learned from studying material and relating it to a particular problem.

The second role performed by the tutor is to *stimulate and maintain a collaborative working atmosphere*. This means ensuring that the conditions exist that allow effective study and collaboration. To do this, the tutor must consider the following points:
- What is the level of participation by each group member?
- Is the way of working methodical?
- Can everyone take part in the discussion?
- How is the discussion leader managing his / her tasks?
- Do other group members allow the discussion leader to fulfil his / her duties?

The tutor provides a sort of back up or safety net for the discussion leader. Prior planning and regular evaluation of the tutorial group, with respect to both the content and the process, will enable the tutor to optimise group functioning.

There are a number of ways in which the tutor can conduct these responsibilities. Tutor performance is based on personal qualities, expectations of the module and student capabilities, attitudes towards the processes of teaching and learning and experience with problem-based learning. Tutors may not be conversant with every aspect of the study material contained within a particular module. This may affect the performance of the tutor in the group. The tutor can also be influenced by the way in which a tutorial group functions.

Students will get to know various tutors during their studies. Some tutors will pay more attention to the group process than others and some will urge their students to study the material more intensively than others. And some tutors, of course, will be more likable than others.

A new module not only means a new tutorial group, but usually a new tutor. When a new tutorial group comes together, group members will have had a wide range of different experiences of previous tutors. This means they will probably have different expectations of how a tutor should operate within the group. For example, some group members will be used to a tutor who wants to know straight facts, some will be used to a tutor who explains the material without allowing the students to fully grasp or explore everything, and some will be used to a tutor who has made no effort to contribute any content. The students will need some time to get accustomed to a new tutor's approach to the tutorial.

There is no such thing as the ideal tutor. After all, tutors are only human. Nevertheless, we would like to end this chapter with an image of the tutor we believe might function optimally within the tutorial system. This tutor believes the most important thing is to allow the student to study as independently as possible. The tutor sees himself not primarily as a provider of information and does not impose personal knowledge and expert standards on the students, but helps them to find their own level within a particular field of study. A good tutor will listen, ask questions and point students in the right direction. He will relate to the students' existing level of knowledge and encourage them to overcome the hurdles confronting them. His major tasks will be to stimulate the formulation of ideas, explanations and hypotheses and to ask regularly for alternative explanations. To be effective, the tutor will keep track of the students' progress and test their understanding of the subject matter. He will ensure that the students are working actively on the subject-matter central to the module.

The tutor stimulates a collaborative atmosphere within the tutorial group and encourages students to adopt a methodical approach as the best means of achieving the intended learning objectives. In short, this tutor not only knows *how* to participate but also *when* and *when not* to intervene.

4 Individual study skills

4.1 Introduction

Problem-based learning places different demands on students in a number of respects but particularly with regard to independent study skills. So, it is important to recognise these differences and try to develop appropriate strategies for dealing with them.

Students on a problem-based course need to be highly independent in their study habits. In problem-based education, the number of hours set aside for independent study is generally greater than for other forms of learning. The previous chapters have concentrated mainly on the joint activities carried out *between* students. These activities provide the platform on which to build *individual* study as ultimately learning remains an individual process where *you* have the major responsibility.

The aim of this chapter is to deal with those aspects of independent study specific to problem-based learning that are unfamiliar to most students. The chapter will focus on a number of means that can be used to structure your independent study activities. We concentrate on the way in which you can select and study your learning materials and also on how to create a *study plan*, manage a *study documentation system* and prepare for *exams*. As this book can only provide a limited amount of information, we have included a list of recommended reading at the end of this book to help you find more detailed information and advice on a variety of relevant subjects.

It takes time to develop a consistent approach to study that matches well with the method of education with which you are working. The aim of this book is to set you on the right course. You should also critically examine the way in which you study on an ongoing basis. Situations may change and different demands will be made on you, necessitating a change in your working style. By constantly re-evaluating your learning strategies you will 'learn how to learn', a process that will stand you in good stead in your professional career, where situations change constantly.

4.2 Selecting learning resources

One characteristic of problem-based learning is that students approach their individual studies from a specific set of learning objectives. As a result you will need to access a variety of different *learning resources*. This way of working differs somewhat from the more traditional approach, where students are expected to systematically work their way through one textbook (usually dealing with a single discipline). In a problem-based programme you have to utilise a number of different learning resources simultaneously. You need to learn to make sense of the different learning materials and select from them carefully and appropriately to fulfil your learning objectives. The learning objectives provide you with the framework to acquire knowledge and insight into the particular topics you have chosen to study as well as various related disciplines and important theories and principles associated with them.

When working towards learning objectives, you will have to search for new information. When you are faced with a problem, it will be unusual for you to be given a direct reference to a specific book chapter. You will be asked to choose what to study for yourself. The question you need to ask is 'How can I make the most effective choices?'

You should realise that you will often have to consult a variety of sources or search through a number of book chapters to meet the objectives set in the tutorial group. Besides books and journals, there are other sources of information to consult such as videotapes, computer simulations and teaching staff.

Clearly formulate the information you need and don't be put off track by all kinds of other information you happen to come across in your searches. If you want to find something about a particular subject, it is useful to clearly define the terms (or keywords) you will be using when searching for information on this subject. Defining these keywords accurately and comprehensively will give you a good foundation from which to find the resources you require. Sometimes it will prove difficult to find precise sources, simply because you are not familiar with all the terminology. A good quality dictionary, thesaurus or encyclopaedia will be of great benefit in helping you to search efficiently and effectively.

In the early stages of your studies it is hard choosing learning resources successfully, so you will often be provided with additional guidance. The module book usually lists a number of important books and other learning aids. Sometimes you will be given a collection of articles from the literature. Start your searches here and build on from them (e.g. using cross-references from the texts provided). You will normally be provided with a *recommended reading list* in your first year, specifying the books that will be essential for this period of study. Make sure that you buy these books or that you have access to them from a library.

If you're still stuck, search the *library* for suitable resources. Most academic libraries now have a computerised cataloguing system incorporating various search options. You will soon learn that searching for information is a vital skill and understanding how literature is classified is an important part of this. Slowly but surely, a picture will begin to emerge of the various components of your field of study and of the books that contain useful information. It is important for you to become proficient in searching catalogues at an early stage. Read through the instructions provided by the library, attend training sessions and don't be afraid to ask for help.

Many libraries also have facilities for consulting journal articles and reports either via a local computer system or through Internet access to information databases. Make sure you familiarise yourself with the search programmes used locally so that you can find relevant information quickly.

Once you have identified potential study resources, you should find out whether the information you are looking for can in fact be found in those books or journals. There is little point in reading through a book and then coming to the conclusion that you have not achieved the learning objectives you set yourself. The following tips are intended as pointers for selecting information.

- Try to form an opinion on the suitability of a book or article in *5 to 10 minutes*, taking the following into account.
- Find out what the book is about and who it has been written for. Read the title, the text on the jacket flap and the foreword or abstract. As a first year student you will be particularly interested in sources that provide an introduction to a particular subject. Descriptions such as 'Text book on ....', 'An Introduction to....' or 'Student edition', generally provide a good indication. Later on in your course you may need to select more specialised texts.
- Is the book up-to-date? Look at the publication date and quickly check the dates in the reading list. In most studies, you will want the most recent information. Books older than ten years should be viewed with caution.
- Look at the relevant pages containing the information you need. Consult the index, glossary or table of contents. In the case of journal articles, where there is often no contents page, we recommend that you glance through the headings and sub-headings.
- Read the first page or abstract of the selected section. You should do this to see whether you can follow the argument. If not, it would be wise to try looking for another source initially.

Similar principles could be applied to other materials such as computer-assisted learning packages or videos.

4.3   Studying texts

Once you have established that a chapter or article is worth looking at, you are faced with the task of digesting the material. This is the crux of your study activities. The first thing you're interested in is whether you will be able to achieve your learning objectives by reading a particular text. Having selected a longer text, e.g. a whole chapter or article, it is still advisable to first browse through the text, using the following framework:

- Read the summary or the conclusions at the end of the passage selected.
- Read the paragraph headings and pay attention to bold or underscored sections of text.
- Examine tables, diagrams and illustrations.

If, having done so, you feel you are on the right track then read the text again thoroughly. Don't simply dismiss these initial steps as a waste of time. Browsing through the text will enable you to form a general impression of the contents of the text and have an objective in mind. It will make detailed reading of the text a lot easier.

When reading through the text, keep asking yourself if the information helps you understand the problem. It's not just a question of being able to turn up at the next tutorial meeting with a number of explanations or findings. It's important to learn the most important aspects and write them down so that you can remember and refer back on them at a later stage. You should not be satisfied with simply having found the answer to a question. It is important, as in other forms of education, to study the texts and understand the contents thoroughly, and be able to recall and elaborate on the information. The problem-based method focuses on creating conditions that enable you to achieve this. Learning within a specific context (i.e. related to a specific issue or problem), is often more effective than gathering facts and insight by consulting study materials in isolation (i.e. unrelated to a specific context). If you put your existing knowledge to use when analysing a problem, set your own learning objectives and select your own the learning material, you will be approaching new learning materials far more effectively.

Engaging actively with your study material means that you are trying to test your understanding of what you are reading. You're also trying to find out whether your reading is actually leading you to a better understanding of the problem. This doesn't just mean finding definite answers to specific questions. It means that you will follow up other learning opportunities in related aspects of the literature. A good way of immersing yourself in material is to set yourself questions concerning the text you've just read. For example, you might ask yourself whether the explanations given in the text are related to the subject matter discussed in the tutorial group. Was the tutorial on the right track? Perhaps there are alternative explanations? Is the content of the text at odds with what you've read elsewhere on the subject? (This question occurs more often than you'd imagine!) Do you understand the jargon? Can you follow the reasoning in the text? Importantly, after finishing the text, are you able to summarise it in your own words?

If there's something you don't understand, try to find an answer in the text. Sometimes you might have to consult another book, consult with other members of your tutorial group or with staff to get the answer. If you don't succeed, note down exactly what you don't understand so that you will be able to discuss the matter when you report back to your next tutorial.

Students starting a problem-based course often have difficulty trying to establish the depth to which they must study a particular subject. When you start reading, you will come across many new concepts and interpretations that each have to be looked up. Sometimes you'll feel that a learning objective can only be attained properly when you've managed to trawl your way through the entire literature on the subject. This is not the intention of your course organisers but it does indicate one of the major difficulties you will have as a student on a problem-based learning course. Keep in mind that module organisers have planned the study activities based on the time available between tutorials. It would be impossible to study a long book thoroughly in this time.

The module book will give an indication of what's expected of you. Discuss the study activities with your tutor during your tutorial group meeting to give you a clearer picture of expectations. Your performance in tests and assessments will also enable you to appraise the level of demand being placed on you and in due course you will gain a better understanding of these demands.

4.4   Making notes and diagrams

We have emphasised the importance of taking *notes* several times in this book. Taking notes can help you to engage actively with the learning material. You also need good notes to enable you to report back to the tutorial group. Of course, they are also critical in setting down for yourself the points you consider important to remember at a later stage. You can take notes during your own study, in the tutorial, at lectures and when consulting the experts.

In the course of your studies, you will likely take notes on a large range of topics. Use a new sheet of paper for each new topic so that you can to arrange your material into some sort of order. Make a habit of stating the subject at the top of each sheet, and the date and time on which the notes were made. It is also useful to state the module and problem numbers, i.e. 'Module 1.1, Problem 14'. If you have used other references, clearly write down the title, author and year of publication, as well as the pages consulted and source.

The actual content and detail of the notes is very much up to you. As a guide, however, you should avoid copying out long sections of text. Sometimes students try to get a grip on the subject matter by making overlong summaries and quite often give everything the same importance. A problem with this way of working is that students either don't or only partly discover the meaning of the message that the author has included in his arguments. Try to limit yourself to the main points, definitions, important statistics and interpretations of terms. To help simplify complex items of material, make a *diagram* illustrating the relationship between the most important concepts of a topic. This technique is known as *concept mapping*. Concept mapping is a technique whereby students construct a network linking concepts, which shows the mutual relationships between these concepts. It is important that the relationships between two or more concepts is always given briefly and concisely by using relevant verbs, adverbs (e.g. leads to, administers, in the form of, via, to, through). Box 29 shows a concept map from a text about particulate matter.

This concept map shows at a glance the hierarchical structure of the concepts and their most important relationships. Naturally, not all concept maps can be reduced to such forms. Connections between concepts can often be ambiguous or related to each other in more than one way so that the concept maps will be harder to construct.

The technique of concept mapping has various advantages over the more commonly used techniques of making summaries:
- Concept mapping fits naturally with the way people store information in their memory, namely in network structures. Applying this technique means that you 'learn in a more natural manner'.
- A concept map is a visual representation of information or knowledge. Many people learn visually so a concept map supports this way of acquiring information.
- Concept mapping 'forces' you to process the subject matter actively. By searching for the essential concepts and their mutual relationships you continuously process the subject matter in a meaningful way. This active processing of the subject matter makes it easier to remember and recall the information.
- Concept mapping helps you to see the relationships between what you already know, your prior knowledge and the newly acquired knowledge. From this viewpoint concept mapping is a technique that fits well with the method of problem-based learning.
- Concept maps help you to see the most important concepts and their mutual relationships in a text and to recognise inconsistencies and gaps in texts more easily.
- A concept map is easier than a summary to extend in all directions and change if necessary.
- Concept mapping makes it possible to combine more than one text on the same subject in the same concept map. If you study more than one text for a particular learning objective then using the concept mapping technique means you won't need to repeatedly write out long summaries, but instead you can often the combine the opinions of various authors in one coherent structure as a single concept map.
- A concept map provides a good starting point for reporting back to the tutorial during the phase of synthesis.

Box 29 *Example of a concept map about Ambient Particulate Matter*

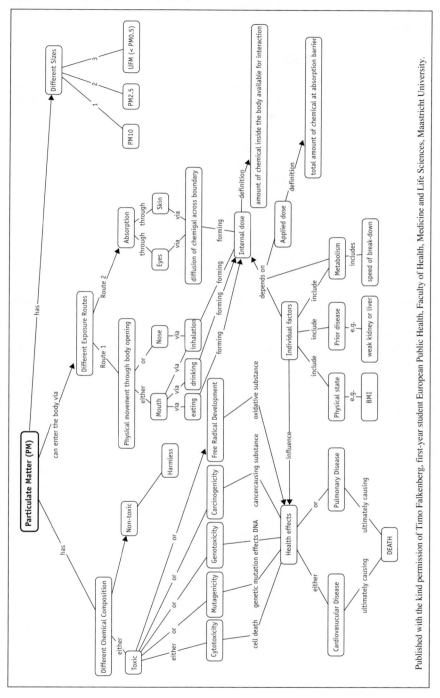

Published with the kind permission of Timo Falkenberg, first-year student European Public Health, Faculty of Health, Medicine and Life Sciences, Maastricht University.

When you make a concept map, bear the following points in mind:
- Identify the most important concepts and note these down.
- Arrange the concepts in order in the map. Begin by picking out one or two key elements as a starting point. Outline each of the key concepts.
  - Try to identify the relationships between concepts. The relationships between concepts are of essential importance if one is to understand the significance of written or oral information properly. Use brief and concise phrases for this. Again, be economical with the number of verbs or other words that you use to describe the relationship. The connections made between the concepts must be meaningful.
  - Leave lots of room so that you can make any additions or modifications.
  - Try to use a clear structure (e.g. hierarchical) and avoid using the same concept more than once in the map.
  - Avoid using lines that cross or are overly long.
  - Try to simplify the map by combining concepts and relations.

Nowadays, there is a wide range of computer programs that allow you to create concept maps electronically. These computer programs have been specially designed for educational purposes. Some advantages of these computer programs are:
- you can change a concept map much more quickly and easily without making a mess of things;
- you can use different fonts, colours, arrows and symbols to create the map;
- some computer programs have graphics and templates that you only need to fill in;
- you can convert a map to different file formats and e.g. insert it as an illustration in Word;
- you can send maps as email attachments to other members of the tutorial group.

In the beginning you will likely find the technique of concept mapping time-consuming and cumbersome, because you are more used to other ways of processing information. Learning how to work with a new technique is always harder because you won't have built up any routine yet and you might have to unlearn other techniques. You first have to learn how to go about concept mapping in a handy way. However, once you have gained some experience with mapping concepts and their mutual relationships you will discover that you are studying your literature much more actively. You will find yourself approaching each new book chapter and every new article with a more inquiring attitude. You will be faster on the look out for the main and secondary points, for the structure lying behind the text and for the relationships between the different concepts in, between and among particular publications. All this will help you learn in a more meaningful way.

4.5 Studying texts in a foreign language

These days, in countries where English is not the main language, higher education programmes regularly use English and other foreign language textbooks. When you search through the available literature, you will regularly come across titles in German, French, Spanish and English. Studying learning materials written in a foreign language may help you at a later stage in your career since specialised literature (e.g. business and academic journals) may be written in different languages.

If this is the case, bear in mind that it will take longer to read and understand foreign-language material simply because your knowledge of that language will be limited. Perhaps you may fail to understand the drift of the arguments properly or you may get bogged down in complex sentence structures.

You will have to get used to the idea that reading a newspaper or novel in a foreign language, which you may have been used to at school, is completely different to studying an academic text written in a foreign language. This is not just because of different use of language and terminology, but also because you are expected to relate the content to the knowledge you have already acquired on the subject. Once you have translated a passage of text, you will have to ask yourself what you are going to do with the new information.

Here are a few useful tips for when you begin studying texts in a foreign language for the first time:
- Make sure you have a good *dictionary* handy. Most general bilingual dictionaries will not contain definitions of specialised terminology. You will often find source language dictionaries and glossaries on the subject or specialist bi-lingual dictionaries in the library.
- Avoid these two *extremes* when looking up definitions.
  1 Do not look up everything you are not sure about. The time you spend on translation will be at the expense of time that you could usefully take to study.
  2 Do not rely on guesswork, otherwise you will end up inventing your own work. The chances of a misunderstanding occurring are much greater.
- If you do not understand the meaning of the sentence, start by looking a word up in the dictionary. If there are a number of unfamiliar words, start with the verb, then the nouns. If you're still unsure, look up the rest of the words in the sentence.
- Write down specialist terms on a separate piece of paper. This will come in useful at a later stage and prevent your having to look up the word again.
- If your knowledge of a specific language is limited, it is wise to list the definitions of all the most commonly occurring words.

This procedure will take some time, but you should remember that not only will your knowledge of the subject improve, your proficiency in the foreign language will too. Try to keep the two aspects separate. Once you have *translated* a passage, you will have to *study* it. Ask yourself if the passage you have read contributes to your understanding of the subject. After all, the main aim of studying a text is to improve your knowledge of the subject.

If you start realising that you are having more trouble understanding foreign texts than your fellow students, spend more time trying to improve your command of that language. You can do this by spending more time on foreign texts as well as by reading novels, magazines or newspapers. The most important advice that can be given is to practice reading foreign languages more.

4.6   Recording your studies

Study methods in problem-based education entail acquiring knowledge about all kinds of subjects from different study sources. Seldom will you read a book from cover to cover, tending usually to pick out one or two chapters before moving on to the next publication. This method of working means that you will have to keep a note of everything you've read. Within a particular module, you'll probably be able to remember all the reference material you've studied on a specific subject and the tasks for which you've made notes. However, after a number of modules you'll start to forget. Make sure you are in a position to quickly find the reference material again. It will be easier for you to remember previous study by reading through notes made previously or re-reading texts you've already studied.

The aim of recording what you have studied is to provide you with an overview of the information you've managed to gather so far. This could be called your personal *documentation system*. Make sure that the information is arranged in such a way that you can find things easily again.

Building up your own *mini library* of books that you frequently need to refer to is another important way of augmenting the record of your studies. In problem-based education, it is a mistake to think that you will be able to make it solely with taking your own notes from borrowed books (and maybe a few photocopies). If you have your own textbooks, you will be able to make notes in them and will always have them close at hand. In time, you will get to know the structure and content of the most frequently used books, which means you will need to invest less time documenting your studies. Money spent on a good, well chosen reference work is never wasted.

Your personal documentation system includes the module books, off-prints, your own notes from different subjects, test results and other material relating to your studies such as essays.

To make your documentation system really useful, it should be arranged systematically. There are many ways of organising the system. In an ideal situation you would have a system based on keywords so that you can find anything directly relating to a subject. Those of you with a personal computer might consider using an electronic card-index system. However, there is an argument against setting up the perfect index system: it is laborious and time-consuming. Having a clear picture of all the needed keywords will help you to create a workable system. It won't be possible to cover a complete range of subjects under a single heading. After studying part of the learning material, you will undoubtedly come across new keywords that need to be added to your documentation system. You'll have to weigh up the time and energy needed to do this against the user-friendliness of such a system. One thing is certain however: some order in your system is essential, otherwise you'll waste too much time looking for the information you need. There is no ideal system. It depends on your personal preferences and habits. Also important are the nature of the study programme and the structure of the field of study in question. There are no hard and fast rules. To help you, however, we have listed a few suggestions for how to go about the task.

A module-based system
Many systems are based on the principle that you tend to remember a particular subject according to the module in which it was originally studied. Keep all the bits and pieces of information dealt with in a module (e.g. notes, photocopies and marks) in a separate folder or file. Sometimes you will have made notes in your module book referring you to the material available. You might wish to make a table of contents at the front of your file.

A subject-based system
These systems always require a keyword-related structure. Larger versions require a card-index system showing exactly where the relevant information can be found. In simpler versions you can try categorising the information per subject in separate files.

Combined systems
Some students set up a system based on the educational modules and then transfer the information regarding a subject to the most recent module in which the subject was dealt with.
Sometimes, the information on specific subjects is linked to specific textbooks. Brief notes made in the book refer to the folders containing the additional information.

4.7   Time management

We have already emphasised that problem-based education demands a great deal of self-sufficiency on the part of the student. You will frequently be required to make your own study schedules and plans. When you first come into contact with this method of learning, you will probably get the impression that you have lots of spare time. This is partly true because the number of hours of contact learning (tutorials, lectures, practical work, etc.) is less than in other forms of education. Commonly, two-hour tutorial meetings are held twice a week in addition to the eight or ten hours devoted to practical work, training sessions and lectures. For much of the week, therefore, you will be left to your own devices, but you must remember to devote much of this time to self-study. In most higher-education study programmes teaching staff expect students to study for about 40 hours per week. So in problem-based education with 12-14 hours committed to tutorials and other activities on the timetable this leaves about 26-28 hours for independent work. This may vary in practice, of course, but you should assume that this is roughly the amount of time you will need.

You will naturally have a great deal of freedom to choose the time you want to spend on self-study. In practical terms, however, the times planned for tutorials will largely determine the way in which you plan your study activities. Each week, you will be expected to achieve your learning objectives and, as such, you will have to develop some kind of routine for yourself. Of course, you will also have to take into account your other commitments for the week, such as lectures and practical work. Finally, there will be other work, such as essays and assignments that you will not be able to complete in less than a couple of days and for which you need to schedule time.

Before commencing a new module it is advisable to draw up a rough timetable of your study plans to avoid any unpleasant surprises along the way. The way you fill in your time depends very much on yourself. Some students like to get up at the crack of dawn, while others prefer to work late in the evening. You need to identify the most productive times for you and make the most of these. Personal commitments also play a part in the way you allocate your time. Students have a social life too, employment commitments or simply want a weekend off. Studying effectively means striking a balance between these activities.

Other things you should take into consideration are library opening times and the times available for carrying out your practical work. Sometimes you will have to adapt your times to fit in with other students who also want to make use of facilities. Make sure you don't waste unnecessary time going back and forth from your accommodation to other sites on the campus.

No doubt it will take a while to get used to this way of working. However, finding a routine in your study activities is not something you should take too lightly.

A *time management* system will enable you to make a rough assessment of your study schedules and will give you a basis on which you can modify them if necessary. Make a note of how you spend your time in the coming week. Use a timetable as illustrated in box 30. Several times per day jot down on the timetable what you've been doing in the preceding few hours. Don't leave it until the very last minute in the evening, because you will eventually forget and the effect will be lost. Try to be as honest with yourself as possible and remember that the goal is to improve your own personal effectiveness.

Categorise your activities according to the following examples:

a   Planned teaching activities, such as tutorials, training sessions, practical work and lectures;
b   Self-study activities in the library or at college;
c   Self-study activities at home;
d   Travelling;
e   Personal care: eating, sleeping, etc;
f   Household chores: cleaning, shopping, etc.;
g   Relaxation, e.g. sport, going out or watching TV.

On the back of the timetable, make a note of what you've studied: the name of the book, the subject, how many pages you've read and how much time you've taken. After filling in the list you will be in a better position to answer the following questions about the way you spend your time.

- Are there specific times during the day when you are more productive? Why should you be more productive at these times?
- What were your expectations regarding the way you spend your time and your productivity? Does your time record sheet show whether you have attained these expectations?
- What are the most important causes of you wasting time?
- What made you run out of time?
- Can you identify any factors that interfere with your productivity?
- Can you identify any factors that help you study?
- Do you have a balanced schedule across the categories? Can you change it in any way?
- Are there any essential activities (either personal or for your studies) that you are simply not managing to include in your timetable?

In the tutorial you might agree to record the way you spend your time for the coming week and discuss it at the next meeting. This will give you an idea of how others use their time and you'll be able to share experiences and ideas.

Box 30 *Example of a weekly time-management scheme*

Time	Monday date:	Tuesday date:	Wednesday date:	Thursday date:	Friday date:	Saturday date:	Sunday date:
07.00 – 07.30							
07.30 – 08.00							
08.00 – 08.30							
08.30 – 09.00							
09.00 – 09.30							
09.30 – 10.00							
10.00 – 10.30							
10.30 – 11.00							
11.00 – 11.30							
11.30 – 12.00							
12.00 – 12.30							
12.30 – 13.00							
13.00 – 13.30							
13.30 – 14.00							
14.00 – 14.30							
14.30 – 15.00							
15.00 – 15.30							
15.30 – 16.00							
16.00 – 16.30							
16.30 – 17.00							
17.00 – 17.30							
17.30 – 18.00							
18.00 – 18.30							
18.30 – 19.00							
19.00 – 19.30							
19.30 – 20.00							
20.00 – 20.30							
20.30 – 21.00							
21.00 – 21.30							
21.30 – 22.00							
22.00 – 22.30							
22.30 – 23.00							
23.00 – 23.30							
23.30 – 24.00							
24.00 – 00.30							
00.30 – 01.00							

4.8   Exams, finals and course assessment

Nowadays, almost all courses incorporate continuous assessment schemes where marks are awarded at the end of each successfully completed module. The way in which marks are tied in with studying differs from course to course. Sometimes marks are linked to exams taken at the end of each module. In other cases, however, points can be awarded on the basis of participation in practical work, the completion of assignments or a presentation.

In view of the fact that courses differ widely in the way in which they formulate their system of exams, this book can only give a few general tips on this subject.

- Carefully read through the information on how your course is assessed (i.e. course work and exams) and do not hesitate to ask questions if you are unsure of certain things. Remember to take into account any additional obligations such as work assignments, oral presentations, practical work, attendance requirements in tutorials and what happens when you're prevented from attending part of the exam.
- Read up exactly on how marks can be attained.
- Before taking your first 'real' exam, have a look at previous ones to gain an impression of the kind of questions that might be asked. Some courses make this information available or arrange 'mocks'. You can usually ask students further on in your course for information on exams from previous years.
- In addition to marks, the exam result is usually accompanied by detailed information regarding the questions that you answered correctly or incorrectly, plus the overall results for that year. Use this information to your advantage as feedback on your study activities. This way you will be able to find out where you may have been too complacent, what study material you have not understood clearly and how your results compare with others in the group.
- In problem-based learning you may find that you have conducted up-to-date research providing information that is contradictory to established textbooks. Using such information in an exam may result in you being marked-down inappropriately. If you feel that this is the case you should bring the supporting evidence to the attention of the exam committee. This will enable them to judge the evidence for themselves and, if necessary, make appropriate refinement to the assessment process.
- If your exams results are unsatisfactory, find out when and where you will be able to do the retakes.

4.9   Learning issues

Many students value problem-based learning methods. Surveys of students at the University of Maastricht show that a large proportion of students have indicated that problem-based learning is actually their main reason for choosing to study there. Courses using problem-based learning methods have lower dropout ratios and shorter study periods. However, these positive results do not mean that everyone can cope with the challenges raised by this method of learning.

Not all students have the necessary level of self-discipline to plan and implement their own study activities. This might lead to them devoting too little time to their studies. Other students may feel insecure because they are not told exactly what to study. Others simply do not like working in a tutorial-based atmosphere. Inevitably, some students will reach the conclusion that this form of study is not for them.

Having doubts about your course or the working method is not unusual. After a few months' study, many students will begin to ask themselves whether this form of education can fulfil their initial expectations. You will need to decide whether you can address the issues satisfactorily. Talk the issues through with your fellow students and tutors. This may help you to plan your studies better, help you to identify major problems and generate specific ideas for how to deal with them. It is common for students to experience difficulties early on in the course that can be resolved with early attention. If you have problems with specific aspects of your studies, try to pay more attention to the subject in question.

4.10   Learning to learn

Problem-based education provides a challenging way for students to get to grips with mastering a profession. Adopting an active approach to your own learning is not only a good way of helping you attain qualifications, it also provides a basis on which to build your future career. Academic and vocational study programmes deal with professions in which a complex level of knowledge and skills plays an important role. As soon as new areas of knowledge, concepts and techniques become important, the demands placed on such professions will change too. Keeping pace with the changes in your profession is a continuous challenge. What problem-based learning can provide is an opportunity to learn how to acquire new knowledge and skills from the very start of your studies. As well as gaining qualifications, 'learning to learn' is just as important a goal worth aiming at. We wish you every success in reaching this goal.

5   Skills required by tutorial group members

5.1   Introduction

This chapter focuses on the skills students need to enable them to work together effectively in tutorial groups. It is divided into a number of sections, each of which dealing with a specific aspect of working in a tutorial.

5.2   The first meeting in a module

A tutorial group is usually established for the duration of a single module, so students will be confronted with a new group and tutor at the beginning of each module.
Since the composition of the group differs from module to module, the new group will have to agree upon the way to work at its first meeting. To optimise collaboration, it is important to bear the following key aspects in mind.

5.2.1   Get to know each other
You can safely assume that you will encounter a number of new faces in each freshly formed tutorial group, so it is essential to introduce yourself to the rest of the group, including the tutor. As names are often difficult to remember, it can help to write your name on a card and place it on the table in front of you for the first couple of meetings. It is also important to express your expectations and plans for the forthcoming module. Don't take it for granted that every student in the group will have the same focus and background. And if most students come from different programmes and colleges, which usually is the case in international courses, you will need to pay attention to potential differences in expectations. In preparation, we recommend that before the first meeting you read the introduction to the module book and browse through its contents. This will enable you to mention which aspects of the module you find particularly interesting. In addition, you might like to say something about any previous experience in relevant areas and your expectations of working in a tutorial group.

5.2.2   Agree on how the group will work
You need to agree on the order in which group members take on the role of discussion leader and scribe. A simple solution would be to do it in alphabetical order by name. Agree on what action to take if someone is absent for a tutorial. You may decide to exchange addresses, telephone numbers or e-mail addresses so that everyone can be contacted easily. Discuss also the way the group will work during the meetings. Box 31 gives an overview of some important items for discussion and examples of a resulting code of conduct for the tutorial group.

5.2.3   Plan your time

In general, the module book will indicate the rate of progress at which problems should be accomplished. Once you've read the introduction to the module book and read through the problems, you'll be able to form an idea of the labour intensity of the various aspects. Try making a provisional timetable, estimating the rate of progress at which you think the problems can be tackled if this is not specified. The tutor will help you with this. Keep a written record of everything you agree so that you can see whether any changes are needed to the plan after the first couple of meetings. Take into account other activities covered by the module book, such as practical work and lectures. You might have to put your name down for some activities that have restricted attendance.

Box 31 *Example of a code of conduct for a tutorial group*

- *Attendance*. Attending tutorial meetings should be a priority for everyone. If you can't be present it is up to you to find out what happened at a meeting and what agreements have been made about the learning objectives for the next session.
- *Preparation*. Everyone should prepare themselves carefully for meetings. This includes studying learning resources in a meaningful way, e.g. by preparing a concept map, by thinking critically about the resources studied and by preparing questions for discussion. Studying factual knowledge alone is insufficient to participate in the discussion.
- *Communication*. Interaction in the tutorial group should an open and multilateral exchange. Everyone should practice active listening. Group members share their knowledge and findings. Differences in ideas, views or arguments are important; conformity of opinion will not be supported. Group members should focus on finding the best possible explanations or solutions and not become involved in winning a debate.
- *Attitude*. Members should be critical of all contributions (including their own) to the group. However, they should also show respect for the ideas and personal beliefs of others.
- *Procedure*. Members of a tutorial group should not skip any steps in the problem-based learning process. Input of information is important during the analysis phase. That implies removing any barriers obstructing explanations or solutions. Even tentative, rudimentary thoughts about an explanation or solution can be useful. During the synthesis phase less emphasis is placed on factual knowledge. Instead, structuring and applying information as well as critical appraisal become more important. At every meeting the scribe should make a note developments on the backboard.
- *Responsibility*. Everyone is equally responsible for how the tutorial group functions. Decisions are founded on broad-based discussion.

- *Evaluation.* Group members should evaluate the progress of the group regularly. This should include observations and opinions about progress not only on the content level of the subject matter but also on how well the group is collaborating. Personal feedback should not be ignored. Agreements made during the evaluation should be respected and carried out.

5.3   Providing and requesting information

Much time in the tutorial group is taken up with the exchange of information. Managing this information is an important function of the tutorial group so that discussions on a particular problem can be properly channelled and understanding of the study material enhanced. We will consider how important it is to exchange information properly and then make a number of suggestions as to how you can improve the information process within the tutorial group.

Educational psychologists have discovered that the best method of retaining information is to actively request or actively provide an explanation for a particular issue. The impact is increased only if the explanation is properly presented. An explanation consisting of evidence, examples or an interpretation or clarification to the problem will lead to better levels of performance, for both the person providing the explanation and the person requesting it. In providing an explanation loopholes or ambiguities may become evident to the presenter. This might lead to a reformulation of the explanation, presentation of more graphic examples, a review of one's own understanding of the issues and, if necessary, result in the student revisiting the source study material. By comparison, the person trying to follow the explanation will attempt to understand what is being explained and will question whether it ties in with their existing knowledge on the subject. This process will result in a restructuring and refinement of personal knowledge.

Working like this with the information presented within the group will stimulate the learning process. Clearly there is little sense in limiting explanations to the mention of a reference or book that holds the answer to the problem. Likewise, there is no point in quoting directly from a book or from other notes. You should always try to provide full explanations in your own words and encourage others to do likewise. By all means refer to a diagram or a few keywords as an aid, but do the explaining yourself.

In box 32 is a passage taken from the report of a fictitious tutorial group. The problem they are discussing is 'A warm summer's day' (see Chapter 2), in which a thunderstorm is the central theme. The group has studied various literature sources to provide an answer to the following learning objective: 'Does the cause of lightning have anything to do with electricity and how is this electricity generated in the clouds?'

Box 32 *Example of various types of questions*

Claire: It's wrong to say there's a difference in the electrical charges in the clouds. Differences in the electrical charge occur throughout the area of storm, but I'm not altogether sure how the process develops.

Mark: Thunderstorms occur when a change is brought about in the atmosphere after a number of warm days, e.g. when an area of low-pressure meets an area of high-pressure. In the warmer area, moist air rises. These vertical convection flows are unable to rise above the higher mass of air, because it is colder. The warm convection flow…

Steven: *(interrupting)* How's that possible then? I thought colder air was supposed to sink below warmer air?

Mark: Hm, not quite. Look at the overall picture. We're dealing here with huge air masses that collide in the upper layers. This is why thunderclouds can reach up to heights of 10 to 15 km. As the moist warm air rises, it becomes cooler. The moisture changes in structure, first into water droplets and then into ice crystals. I'm pretty sure that when this transition also takes place there is a change in the electrical charge.

Rachel: Yes, that's right. Depending on the size of these raindrops and ice crystals, they become either positively charged or negatively charged. The larger ice crystals are negatively charged and the ice splinters positively. The crystals lose height and the splinters are forced upwards. Due to the turbulence in the upper layers of air, most of the positive charges are in the upper layers and most of the negative charges in the lower layers. Because of the vast amount of cloud formation, however, there are local variations. This means that in the lower layers there are positively charged pockets of air mixing with negatively charged pockets of air.

Claire: Do these differences in charge cause the flash of lighting between the sky and the ground?

Mark: No. I thought that small electrical currents develop in the cloud, each seeking out the path of least resistance. These small flashes of lightning are called pre-charges.

Claire: But even the experts don't agree on the way in which these charges occur. Besides, these charges release enormous amounts of energy. I once read that they measured balls of lighting in America with a charging potential able to supply electricity to a city the size of Chicago for some time. That would solve a few environmental problems caused by power stations.

Tim: How would you harness all that enormous potential?

Chair: Perhaps we ought to solve the problem of the thunderstorm first. Steven?

Steven: OK, these pre-charges create conduction channels which subsequently enable a bolt of lightning to hit the earth.

Claire: But first there's a flash of lightning from the ground to the cloud?

> *Steven:* The ground is negatively charged, but is a poor electrical conductor. Because of the enormous negative charges in the clouds, however, positive charges occur locally on the ground. When there is a difference in tension between the ground and the lower part of the cloud, the ground might emit a flash of lightning to the cloud. The channels I mentioned previously have already formed within the cloud, which enables the charge to be transmitted downwards with enormous heat and power, eventually hitting the ground.

We will use this sample discussion to demonstrate that providing information can take two forms. Information can consist of factual data, but it can also be a subjective opinion on a particular subject. Often it is difficult to single out information that is *objective and factual* from information that reflects the *personal opinion* a speaker may have of a particular subject. This difficulty comes about because people are inclined to express an opinion as if it were factual information. If we take an example from the extract above, we see that Mark says, 'I thought that…' which would indicate that he is not fully sure of how the process of shifting masses of clouds develops (and you too may have your doubts about the assertion he makes).

Often both the objective and opinion aspects are interwoven, particularly in discussions where personal involvement is concerned. To filter out the factual information from personal opinions, it's important to listen carefully and, where appropriate, ask the person providing the information where he got it from. In this way you will avoid remembering inadequate or incorrect information. During the discussion it is also important not to stray away from the original issue. This is a common problem in group discussions. Jumping from one subject to the next will prevent systematic analysis of a problem or a productive discussion of the study material. Uncertainties about the discussion topic may also arise if those taking part do not fully understand each other, or if the topic is interpreted from a personal point of view. This can lead to a situation in which the participants claim to have understood one another, whilst they are actually talking at cross-purposes. This is why it is important that the information provided relates directly to the subject matter dealt with previously in the discussion.

There are a number of guidelines that might help you to do this:
- Try to pick up on the listeners' way of thinking and be responsive to this.
- Express yourself clearly. Poorly structured sentences and a boring delivery make it difficult for listeners to maintain their concentration. Also take into account the potential receptive capacity of your listeners and don't put too much information into one sentence or introduce unrelated ideas at the same time. Organise your message into key points and secondary points.
- Consider using visual aids (e.g. the board) to help you get the message across.

- When speaking, look at your listeners from time to time and try to read from their faces whether they are still following you.
- Make it clear whenever you're expressing a personal interpretation of a particular text that you've studied. Give a summary of the text as objectively as possible. Refer to the sources on which your view is based.
- Allow other group members to ask questions and don't feel threatened when they do so.
- Summarise the main points of your presentation.

Following these guidelines is not as easy as you might think. Some practice might help, e.g. thinking at home beforehand about the best way of presenting the material you've studied. Making notes, concept maps or diagrams will all help you to inform your group correctly. Try to explain what you've learned in your own words.

The other side of the coin is *asking* for information. By asking questions, new openings in the discussion may appear which had not been apparent previously. It is important to differentiate between *open* and *closed questions*. The questions posed by Tim and Steven in the extract are open questions that provoke a deeper analysis of the problem. Open questions stimulate elaboration. Elaboration means that the information being provided will be enriched so that it becomes easier for listeners to remember. Closed questions always involve one or two alternatives from which the person answering must choose. This can be 'yes' or 'no' or a limited number of categories of answers. To illustrate, assume that Claire asked the following question:

Claire: Is it true that thunderstorms occur more frequently in coastal industrial belts?

In theory, you would expect a 'yes' or 'no' answer to the question ('yes', being the correct answer in this case). Closed questions are not conducive to keeping discussions going and may give rise to a question and answer dialogue. Closed questions do of course provide a means of knowing whether you've interpreted the information correctly.

In the tutorial group both types of questions are important to the conduction of discussion along lively, structured and concrete lines. The emphasis, however, should be on open questions since they will lead to in-depth discussion of the study material. So ask questions that stimulate thinking and debate on the plausibility of the arguments.
Here we present guidelines for facilitating the questioning process in the tutorial group:
- *Does the question relate to the discussion topic?*
  Just as can happen when information is being provided, questions might stray from the topic.

- *Is the question recognisable as a question?*
  Some individuals conceal their questions in the form of an opinion formulated on a particular issue which makes it unclear to the other participants whether the individual is actively contributing to the discussion or simply trying to find out what the others think. Explicit questions always begin with a query such as 'who', 'what', 'why', 'when' or 'how'. This structure indicates to others that a question is being asked.
- *Is the question clearly and concisely formulated?*
  Do not use complicated sentence structures that are likely to distract the person being addressed.
- *Is the question ambiguous?*
  The most common mistake is to ask two or more questions simultaneously. This might result from a poorly formulated question or a need on the part of the questioner to ask as many questions as possible at the same time. The person answering will often not know which question to answer or in what sequence to answer. Nor will that person be capable of remembering all the questions or will otherwise produce an answer which, intentionally or unintentionally, is biased.

Of course many of these rules are followed intuitively. Nevertheless, in assessing the functioning of the tutorial, it is a useful exercise to check whether participants are putting their questions to each other in an effective way.

5.4   Active listening

In a tutorial group that functions well, only one person will be doing the talking at any one moment. Other group members will be listening. At least this is what we assume they will be doing. After all, the fact that someone remains silent during a discussion doesn't necessarily mean that they are listening.
There are always two sides involved in the listening process, namely the speaker and the listener. If ambiguities or misinterpretations arise in the discussion, these may originate in either individual. The speaker can only express a selection of what he is able or wishes to present on the basis of personal knowledge and experience. The listener is in much the same situation and can only interpret the speaker according to personal knowledge and experience. The listener too will be selective in receiving information. The result can be that the listener misinterprets the speaker or is unable to pick up the intended thread of the argument.
Listening can be made difficult by other causes. The listener can be led astray by his own thoughts. He can drift off and not pay enough attention to what is being discussed. Many listeners are fully engaged in thinking about an answer before the speaker has finished. They will miss large parts of information from the speaker. Consequently their reaction only concerns a part what has been said. Listeners also often have the tendency to focus on details, rather than listening to the core of the remarks made by the speaker. Some listeners believe they know

what the other person is going to say after they have heard just a few sentences. They anticipate the thought processes of the speaker and interpret more what the speaker intended to say rather than what he actually said. This results in a great deal of interference in the mutual communication. Speakers have to explain their point again, can react somewhat irritably, give up, or in their turn listen poorly to other speakers. In short, pseudo-interaction occurs and group members react more to each other from their own worlds and manners of thinking rather than trying to really understand the opinions and viewpoints of others. The learning results in a tutorial group become severely damaged by this, because group members understand one another not at all or only partially, communication remains superficial and the desire to follow the contributions made by others decreases. Active listening to what someone has to say or is attempting to say is of real importance for good communication and interaction in a tutorial group.

Actively listening to the contributions of your fellow group members is a skill that can help reduce or eliminate communication problems. Active listening implies a positive attitude towards what the speaker says and a willingness to look for alternative interpretations. Below are a number of tips that will help you to listen actively to the contributions of others in your tutorial group.

- *Maintain regular eye contact with the speaker.* Gestures and facial expressions provide you with additional information about the point that is being made.
- *Concentrate on what the speaker is saying.* Many individuals are inclined to start formulating their own arguments after just a few sentences of a presentation, thus missing out on part of the information provided or the whole picture.
- *Check whether you have fully understood what the speaker has said.* Do this by saying something like, 'If I understand you correctly, you mean…' or asking questions. In this way the speaker gets the chance to confirm, deny or elaborate what has been said.
- *Show that you are listening.* An expressionless face is likely to make the speaker feel uneasy. Respond with a nod or a smile. Don't sit there fiddling with a pencil or staring out of the window.

Speakers can make listening difficult too, e.g. by poorly formulating sentences or speaking in a monotonous tone. Problems can also arise in situations where the speaker takes insufficient account of the needs of listeners by presenting too many arguments at the same time.

5.5   Making summaries

Tutorial groups are characterised by working through a lively exchange of ideas and opinions. Facts, suppositions, arguments and interpretations tumble over and through each other during the phases of analysis or synthesis. From time to time many group members will find to hard to see the wood from the trees. It is difficult to absorb all the information at once or filter out certain aspects, especially when a new subject is being discussed. Information is only truly retained if the relationship between the information and its meaning is fully understood. This is why the information under discussion needs to be put into order on a regular basis. Summarising is an important tool for maintaining the structure and progress of the discussion.

A *summary* is a brief synopsis of (part of) a discussion. It contains the essence of the facts and ideas presented by group members. It can bring order into the multitude of expressed opinions. It can mark the core concepts and explicitly separate the major and secondary points. A summary allows the group to consider its progress and gives members a chance to check whether their contribution has been fully understood. For some participants a summary is the method for testing whether they have fully understood the previous discussion.

Summaries have other favourable influences on discussions and the learning of group members.
- Summaries compel the members of the group to reconstruct (in silence, for themselves) all that has been said and to analyse whether the points put forward by the presenter are correct. Such moments of quiet reflection let members of the tutorial group uncover gaps in explanations or solutions more easily. Unclear points in a summary, therefore, often give rise to further discussion or pose more questions.
- Summaries keep the discussion on track. This makes it easier to see if any member of the group or the group as a whole is getting lost.
- Asking if you may summarise what has been said (at great length) can be a subtle way of halting a presenter who does not know when to stop.
- Summaries make it easier to keep the discussion going in a natural manner after a disruption.
- Summaries often form a natural end to either part of or the whole discussion as such.

Making summaries are, therefore, useful tactics in a discussion. They should take place regularly during group meetings. But despite the fact that summaries can function as a sort of lubricating oil for the discussion you should be careful not to over-use them. Giving too many summaries can be very irritating and may be unnecessary interruptions which frustrate the members of the discussion.
There are no hard and fast rules for the best moment to make a summary. It depends strongly on the difficulty of the information under consideration, the quantity of that information and the physical condition of the group members. If participants are tired and lack concentration, e.g. there will be a greater need for summaries. A suitable moment for a summary is always when a particular part of the subject has been dealt with.

Summaries are by no means the sole prerogative of the discussion leader. Any participant in the discussion (including the tutor) can provide a summary. In general, it can be said that it is more important that summarising takes place than that this should be specifically allocated to the discussion leader or the members of the group. The most natural way is when members of a tutorial group, including the discussion leader, summarise at a suitable moment. However, it is task of the discussion leader to ensure that summaries are given at regular intervals.

Here are a number of tips for making summaries:
- Allow the other group members to *recognise* that you wish to provide a summary. Start by saying things like: 'If I were to give the main points of the discussion...'; 'So, in a nutshell...'; 'Let's recap on what we've just been discussing...'
- Concentrate on *principle thoughts*. A summary may be brief, but it still has to contain the most important contributions of each person taking part in the discussion.
- A summary is a good way of *rounding off* a topic. Once participants have made a number of points in the discussion, they may start becoming repetitive. For this reason, a summary is a good means of bringing an issue to a close. A good time for a summary is when the attention span of the participants is waning. A summary may also provide the group with a way of getting out of a blind alley and give flagging members of the group the chance to feel involved in the discussions again.
- For a particularly difficult concept it may be useful to produce a visual summary using a *board or flipover*. Set down all the most relevant findings clearly and concisely, preferably using keywords.

5.6   Taking notes

During the tutorial meeting each student makes notes for himself about the topics discussed and the decisions taken, e.g. which learning objectives should be studied. After all, without such notes it would be difficult to know what you have to study between the tutorial meetings.

It is often handy to be able to visualise the information discussed by the whole group. A note-taker or scribe is appointed during a tutorial group meeting to support the learning activities. The scribe's activities ensure that important remarks don't just disappear and that a framework of the way the group tackles a problem gets recorded.

A scribe notes the different ideas put forward during the analysis phase as well as the learning objectives proposed during further discussion. The board in the tutorial room can best be divided into four sections in order to make the information most clear in visual form. Figure 5.1 gives an example of the use of the board during the analysis phase.

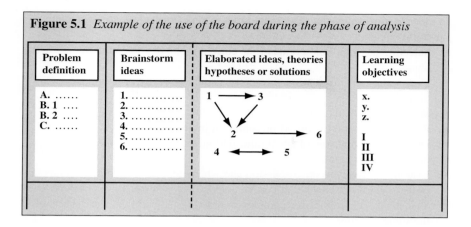

Figure 5.1 *Example of the use of the board during the phase of analysis*

Problem definition	Brainstorm ideas	Elaborated ideas, theories hypotheses or solutions	Learning objectives
A. ...... B. 1 .... B. 2 .... C.	1. .... 2. .... 3. .... 4. .... 5. .... 6.		x. y. z. I II III IV

After reading the problem, its definition as stated by the tutorial group can be noted in the left-hand column (see A, B1, etc.). The ideas arising during the brainstorm phase are noted as keywords (see 1- 6). The largest part of the blackboard is devoted to the next section where the scribe notes the elaboration of these ideas. Diagrams, schemas, mind or concept maps showing descriptions of processes or structures are noted here (see 1 leads to 3, etc.). The final section on the right is for recording posed questions that cannot be answered yet and any big differences of insight that are still unclear or which the tutorial group cannot answer using its previous knowledge (see x, y, z, etc.). These questions and different opinions are the basis for the formulation of learning objectives. Finally, these learning objectives are written out in full in the last section, (see I, II, III, IV).

Using the board like this means all information should get recorded systematically. Recording the contributions reassures members that attention is being paid to their remarks and that their contributions won't be lost. Members of the group will be less inclined to indulge in repetition because it is clear what has already been discussed. When discussion are expressed graphically it becomes easier for group members to summarise and come to unambiguous agreements. Naturally, this way of recording will often not be a simple linear process going from the left to right across the board. Members may want to return to what has been discussed in an earlier phase of dealing with the problem. Then the scribe will have to make new notes in the relevant section of the board. Sometimes certain terms will be used in describing the problem during the first phase that are not completely clear to all students. In that case the scribe should make a note of this at once in the right-hand section of the board so that the members of the tutorial group can include those terms not fully understood in the later phase of formulating the learning objectives. Using the board is a circular process, just as it is in the various paces of the Seven-step method. Students can move backwards and forwards when and if necessary.

In order to function well as a scribe, a student must concentrate on developing the following skills.

- Selecting the important points of the current group discussion to put up on the board.
- Expressing this information succinctly, using keywords, common abbreviations and symbols.
- Writing quickly and legibly.
- Putting information in order; presenting it in diagram form.
- Distinguishing between factual information and personal opinions of the members of the group.
- Listening actively to the discussion and where necessary asking questions in order to clarify or check that you've noted down is correct.
- Visualising (expressing as a graphic or drawing) any still unclear aspects of the subject matter.
- Recording all group agreements, conclusions, and decisions, such as new learning objectives.

The scribe can also fulfil a useful function during the reporting phase, using plans, concept maps or diagrams to organise the results of the self-study carried out by the members of the group. The supportive role of scribe in the learning process of a tutorial group is not specific to a particular member of that group. If students have created their own diagram or concept map during a self-study period, it's a good idea to invite them to put these graphics on the board. Naturally, any changes suggested by other members of the group can then be incorporated.

Appendix 1 of this chapter offers a list which can be used to help observe the skills of various group members mentioned above.

5.7 Evaluating tutorial group meetings

It makes sense to regularly appraise what the tutorial group has accomplished. This review of what the group has achieved and the way in which progress has been made in terms of content and process is called an evaluation. Group members and the tutor can try to identify the causes of any difficulty and agree on a better approach in the future. An evaluation will help give direction to the process of learning in collaboration and provide group members with an opportunity of getting things off their chests. For evaluations to be productive, the following requirements must be fulfilled:

- there must be a specific topic for evaluation;
- each member of the group must have the chance to express an opinion;
- specific decisions must emerge from the evaluation in terms of keeping to or changing agreements, behaviour or rules;
- if a decision is made to change something, the effects of this change must be discussed at the following evaluation.

When a tutorial group decides to evaluate progress, it must do so on the basis of a specific topic. Vague questions, such as 'What did you think of it today?', will lead to vague answers, since group members will not know exactly what 'it' refers to. Does 'it' refer to working through the study material, the group interaction, or the way in which the group discussion was led? It may be totally unclear to some students that this is a specific opportunity to evaluate the tutorial group. Some students may start packing up ready to leave and others may start expressing an opinion based on their own interpretation of the question. More often than not there will be insufficient time to reach any proper conclusions. This can lead to frustrations that might spill over into the following tutorial meeting. To gain a better idea of the views of the group, just one or two topics should be selected and given enough time to be discussed. This will enable group members to respond to each other's ideas and reach agreements on improvements that could be made.

If the tutorial group decides to evaluate the amount of progress made in terms of content, questions should focus on the extent to which the group has succeeded in achieving the goals of the designers of the module. The group will investigate whether their learning objectives and level of integration of the new information is satisfactory, e.g. by asking whether the information acquired matches expectations, whether a sufficient level of study has been performed and relevant learning resources consulted, whether the quality and quantity of knowledge acquired is satisfactory, whether the group has succeeded in attaining an adequate grasp of the study material, and whether or not the tutorial system has provided added value. This kind of review might also relate to the way in which the learning objectives are reported during the meetings or the way in which a sub-theme from the course book has been handled. Decisions can then be taken on how to improve productivity with respect to the content to be covered and the aims of the group on the basis of the evaluation of what has been achieved.

The members of the tutorial group can also discuss the way they work together. Different approaches can be considered during a process evaluation. For example, you can consider whether the group is handling the problems from the course book in a methodical manner, or whether you are all dividing up the work adequately and whether the short and long term planning makes sense. This concerns in particular the procedural side of the cooperation. As well as this, you can discuss the individual contributions of members of the group, the extent of individual participation and what the atmosphere in the group is like, and whether the contributions from members, the discussion leader and tutor are helpful to the development of an open and constructive climate in the group. This concerns in particular the interactional side of the collaboration.

When a tutorial group decides to evaluate its manner of working and progress you can use the following procedure.

- First decide the subject to be evaluated (progress in the subject matter, procedural or interactional manner of working).

- Give everyone the chance to think about this subject and to make brief notes in keyword form about their experiences with that subject.
- Let all members of the group express their opinion.
- Then express your own opinion and ask the tutor for his/her observations and opinion.
- Try to cluster the positive and negative aspects that are put forward.
- Look together for possible improvements and make agreements about changes in behaviour.
- Round off the evaluation with an agreement when to return to this subject to see whether the intended changes have actually led to an improvement.

It is sometimes useful to begin the evaluation by asking group members to fill in a short questionnaire. In this way, individuals can set down their opinions without being influenced by the views of others. The results of the questionnaire can be transferred to the board and used as the basis for further discussion.
It is important to allow the tutor to make evaluating remarks too. The tutor has opportunities to observe the group in action and, on this basis, can make suggestions to improve its progress.

There are no hard rules for when the tutorial group should evaluate itself. This largely depends on the degree of progress made. During the first course, when you start becoming familiar with the concept of problem-based learning, it is advisable to evaluate progress at the close of each tutorial meeting. Thereafter it is useful to do this regularly, after every three or four meetings, or more frequently in the event of problems. The group might also agree to carry out an evaluation in the middle of a tutorial if one of the group members has got bogged down in the content or the process. Holding a time-out like this is best done either directly before or after the break.
Appendix 2 of this chapter offers you a questionnaire for evaluating the various processes, which go on in tutorial groups. The group should decide which part of this questionnaire will be used to discuss progress.

5.8 Providing and receiving feedback

When you evaluate the way of working of a tutorial group, perhaps you'll want to say something about how your fellow group members perform. Feedback is the term we refer to when we want to comment on the performance of others. Feedback is a remark directed at someone containing information on how that person's behaviour is perceived and interpreted. Giving feedback is not an easy task. Many people don't dare tell someone else in public what they think of his behaviour and even less how this behaviour affects them. In your professional work, however, you will often have to give feedback on the behaviour of others. As a manager or a consultant you will often be placed in all sorts of situations where people expect you to give feedback.

When two or more people communicate with each other all sorts of messages take place on a verbal and non-verbal level. Interaction between people is a complex phenomenon in which a great deal can go wrong. People are often not aware of the manner in which they communicate, how their manner of communication is experienced by others and what influence their behaviour has on others. In order to obtain more insight into the way in which you communicate and the effects of your behaviour on other people you can ask those with whom you are communicating for information by asking for feedback about the way in which they perceive your manner of communication.

Giving and receiving feedback during a tutorial can help group members understand more about how they behave themselves and the effect this has on other group members and the mutual cooperation. If conducted well it can increase collaboration in future tutorial work.

The scientists Joe Luft and Harry Ingham, who spent a great deal of time in researching interpersonal feedback, have developed a visual model to clarify the usefulness of giving and receiving feedback. Their model, termed the 'Johari window' after their first names, consists of four quadrants: the public area, the hidden area, the blind area and the unknown area (see Figure 5.2).

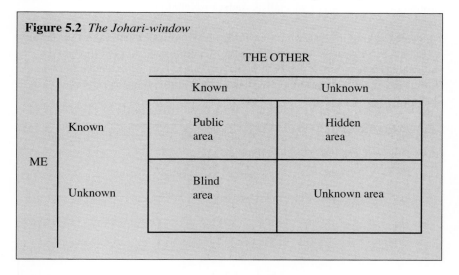

Figure 5.2 *The Johari-window*

THE OTHER

		Known	Unknown
ME	Known	Public area	Hidden area
	Unknown	Blind area	Unknown area

The *public area* is the domain in which my behaviour, emotions or skills are known both to myself and to others. My behaviour is clearly visible to myself and to others in the public area, and both I and the others are aware of it. To give an example: I have the tendency to quickly interrupt other members of the group during group discussion, and both I and the others involved in the discussion know that. Remarks from group members, such as 'Just keep quiet for a moment,' are understood by me at once and, hopefully, accepted.

However, there is also an area within my behaviour, emotions or skills which I am not conscious of, but that others can observe and are aware of. This is the *blind area* or blind spot of the second quadrant. Naturally, I cannot say anything about this area. I simply do not know anything about it, until others make me aware of it. (For the purpose of illustration: when I interrupt someone, I sit forward, making myself bigger than I am, raise my voice somewhat, look intently and point my forefinger at the person I want to interrupt.) Other members of the group can observe this behaviour, but I am not conscious of it myself. My behaviour probably has a certain effect on the other members of the discussion group; they all react to it in some way or another. How they react will differ – one person may retreat into their shell, another might feel challenged, a third may be imitated while a fourth might try to avoid to saying anything in the group.

The third quadrant, the *hidden area*, concerns behaviour that I am aware of but would rather not share with the others. For example: I am very scared of being regarded as a softy in group discussions. So I might put on a hard front and argue my views more strongly than necessary.

Finally, the *unknown area* of the fourth quadrant encompasses what is unknown about me and my behaviour, both to myself and to the others: the unconscious. This area can only be revealed to some extent through particular experiences or through the mediations of specialists such as psychological therapists.

To foster working in a safe and trustworthy environment, a tutorial group should try to increase the range of the public area. According to Luft and Ingham the public area (behaviour known both to me and others) can be extended in two ways: 1. by giving and receiving feedback and 2. through openness. Figure 5.3 illustrates this.

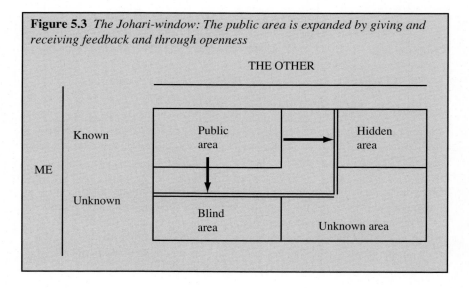

Figure 5.3 *The Johari-window: The public area is expanded by giving and receiving feedback and through openness*

Expansion of the public area by giving and receiving feedback.
When other members of the group tell me something about the way my behaviour comes across to them I get to know myself better (the quadrant of the blind
area becomes smaller). Taking my fictitious tendency to interrupt as an example,
some group members might tell me that they find my non-verbal behaviour
threatening and, if possible, they will avoid entering into discussion with me. If
I keep on interrupting them like this, they will stop paying attention to any of
my contributions. This is not the intended effect of my behaviour! The fact that
not everyone reacts in the same way to my behaviour becomes apparent from
the reaction of someone else in the group. She tells me that my eager interjec-
tions actually stimulate her to push even harder in discussions. Evidently my
disruptive behaviour has varying effects on different members of the group. I
now have to make a decision based on these different bits of information: do I
want to stimulate certain people and frighten off others? Or should I change my
behaviour to something perhaps more friendly and pleasant so that I can keep on
sharing my views with more members of the group and thus increase my sphere
of influence? Feedback presents you with the opportunity to think constructively
about your behaviour in interactions with others and to make conscious decisions
on whether or not to change your course of action.

Expansion of the public area through openness
A second way of expanding the public area is through openness. I can tell others
about something that up till that moment I had kept hidden. In line with the other
example mentioned above, I could tell the others in my group about my fear of
being seen as a softy in discussions. I have armed myself against this by showing
this specific behaviour. Openness means that the hidden area becomes smaller.
Openness, however, does not mean that you have to reveal all your motives,
experiences and emotions to anyone without reservation. Openness means that
when you think it will be useful, you try to pass on information that will promote
the cooperation between the members of the group. When you tell the group
about certain emotions that you experience or certain personal experiences that
directs your behaviour in the group, the other members will understand your
behaviour better and will be able to put this more in perspective.

As mentioned previously, giving feedback is not easy. You've probably experienced people reacting defensively when you've said something about of their
behaviour. Often, this happens because we don't always manage to express an
opinion of someone's behaviour in a way that the other person can handle, e.g.,
when we remark on a person's behaviour in general terms like 'You pretty well
monopolised the discussion today'. People will respond defensively when a
value judgment is being made. Anger, indifference or aggressive behaviour can
also arise if we ignore the feelings of the person receiving feedback or when the
feedback is pedantic, e.g., 'You really should know by now that the discussion
leader is always responsible for...' If you want to avoid defensive reactions you
should adopt a more constructive style of communication. This means backing

off initially, focusing on the problem, treating the other person as an equal and trying to understand his viewpoint.

Effective feedback refers to feedback that can be understood and accepted by the other person and potentially used by that person to modify future behaviour. This can only occur in a situation where both the giver and the receiver of feedback try to understand each other's standpoint and take into account the possible effect their behaviour will have on the rest of the group. This also means that you must both be willing and able to give and take constructive criticism. Some criteria for effective feedback are given below.

- *Take the time to consider what you want to say.* It may help to write down the course of an interesting situation during a discussion for instance.
- You should *describe* the effect the person has had on you. Describing the effect the person had on you means that your comments are not judgemental, interpretative or pedantic. By describing your own feelings and reactions, you are allowing the other person to use the information as he chooses. Give the feedback as *'I'-form messages*, that is, avoid speaking in terms of 'You do this, or that…'. Such remarks all too easily come across as accusing or condemning, so that the feedback misses its target. It is better to use statements like, 'I felt that you interrupted Anna several times, and then you cut in on me. After that I felt unable to make any further contribution.'
- The feedback must be *specific*. Being specific means that you should not voice generalised comments about a group member. Restrict the feedback to what has actually taken place in the contact with this person. Describe your own feelings. By saying that someone is 'overbearing' does not help the other person. It would be better to say, 'When we were about to decide on that particular learning objective, I got the impression you weren't listening at all to what the others were saying. You kept interrupting those who wanted to make other suggestions. I stayed quiet because I felt I couldn't respond adequately, but actually I disagreed with what you were saying.'
- Feedback must be given *at the right moment*, preferably directly after the behaviour that you want to discuss. However, this isn't always possible. First of all, the receiver must want to be given feedback. Second, you cannot always interrupt a discussion to give somebody feedback. What we mean to say here is that the time between the behaviour that you want to comment on and making the comments must not be too long. If this is the case the person showing the particular behaviour often won't remember it anymore, may feel unjustly criticised and become defensive about it.
- Do not hesitate to give *positive feedback* when members of the group show effective behaviour. Giving feedback does not mean that you comment only on the disruptive or dysfunctional behaviour of others. A compliment or positive appreciation gives others the idea that they are making useful contributions to the working method of the tutorial group and stimulates them to show that behaviour more often. It also stimulates people to hear about what they have done well. By bringing somebody's strong points to the fore you show

appreciation for their contribution and the person can build on this behaviour accordingly, and giving positive feedback also makes the giving and receiving of feedback less threatening.

- The other person must also be able to put the feedback to some *practical use*. If you point out the shortcomings beyond a person's own control, frustration will be the only result. Emphasising the positive points of someone's behaviour will increase the usefulness of the feedback. Whenever you identify an issue, always try to suggest a practical solution that would improve the situation. This way the person will get an idea of what they can do to prevent it happening again. Don't restrict yourself to generalities ('I found it rather dull'), but try to make clear what was missing ('You gave hardly any examples') and how it could be improved ('If you'd used a specific example here… would have made it all that much clearer.')
- Feedback must be formulated *in a way which invites a response* from the receiver.

Naturally, receiving feedback comes easiest when you ask for feedback yourself. Then you are clearly interested in the effect of your behaviour on others. When you ask for feedback decide first what exactly do you want to know, and then ask specifically about just that subject. For instance, you might want to know whether the way you explained something in the tutorial group came across successfully to the others. Then try to glean specific information, e.g. whether you separated the main points from the secondary ones, or whether you expressed your ideas clearly, or whether you put too many different topics into one story, or whether you talked in a lively or monotonous tone of voice. A constructive approach to receiving feedback means that you will not immediately rush to defend yourself and give arguments as to why your particular behaviour was so necessary. Listen carefully to what the other group members member have to tell and if you don't understand something ask for further explanation. Invite the people giving feedback to describe as specifically as possible how they perceived and experienced your behaviour. If necessary check if the others have had a similar experience. Try to be open for the comments from your fellow group members and listen to their reactions to your behaviour. Then ask yourself whether your behaviour has the desired effect, is it really what you want or should try to change your behaviour as necessary. Dealing with feedback like this can contribute to better personal functioning in a tutorial group and improve mutual cooperation. Appendix 3 offers a checklist and a plan which can help you to improve your team-working skills.

We started this section by remarking that giving and receiving feedback is not easy. Many students try to avoid it. They find it painful to tell or hear from someone else what is not going so well with the work in the tutorial group. However, giving and receiving feedback does provide more insight into your own communication behaviour and the effect it has on others. It makes you more aware of the blind spots in your own behaviour – actions or skills you might not be so aware of yourself but that others can and do observe. If you are open to feedback you will gain better insight into your own repertoire of behaviour, which enables you to act more professionally in interactions with others.

Appendix: Tools to improve your skills as a tutorial group member

Introduction

In this appendix we offer material which can be used to improve the various skills a student should have for learning in a tutorial group. Developing these skills during your study will not only enhance your own pleasure in study for its own sake, but also the pleasure of participating in an efficient and effective tutorial group. Acquiring high levels of performance in these skills will lead to advantages in your later professional life. The ability to function well in a group is rewarded highly in professional organizations.

The material on offer includes both observation lists as well as checklists. Use these tools on a regular basis to evaluate the progress you yourself, as well as your colleagues, are making in developing proficiency in the skills. Please use the guidelines on giving effective feedback (see near the end of section 5.8) whenever you want to give other members information about their performance in the tutorial group.

Appendix 1 allows you to observe the basic skills members should have for tutorial group meetings.

Appendix 2 allows you to evaluate the various components of discussion in a tutorial group. Feel free to fill in all the components or, your group might agree to score one or two specific components.

Appendix 3 is a checklist for assessing your own levels of performance in tutorial group meetings.

1   Observation list: 'Being a tutorial group member'

General remarks: Jot down in the space provided keywords for the observations you want to give feedback on.

I learnt a lot from my fellow group member(s) (please name):	
I learnt less from my fellow group member(s) (please name):	
I have observed my fellow group members use one or more of the following skills (please tally how often you observed the specific skills in the right-hand column):	
Listening in an active way	
Giving information: • Gives objective facts • Gives personal opinions	
Asking for information • Asks for objective facts • Asks for personal opinions	
Summarises (parts of) the discussion	
Structures bigger parts of the discussion	
Presents subject matter in concrete terms	
Criticises the subject matter or contributions of peers	
Actively visualises the subject matter: concept maps, diagrams, etc.	
Other activities:	

2   A questionnaire for evaluating processes in tutorial groups

The following pages contain a few short lists of questions which can be used to evaluate different aspects of problem-based learning.
- Decide together which list of questions you will use.
- Complete the list of your choice by marking the number that indicates to what extent you agree with the statement. Use the numbers in the following manner: 1 = completely disagree, 2 = disagree, 3 = neither disagree nor agree (neutral), 4 = agree and 5 = completely agree.
- First write down on a separate piece of paper the letter referring to the question (A, B, and so on) and then note your response.
- When everyone is done, write the responses on the board and discuss any noteworthy results.

1
How hard do we really work?

A | 1 2 3 4 5 | I spend sufficient time studying the learning objectives.
B | 1 2 3 4 5 | If there is something that I cannot find immediately, I wait for the next meeting to see if others will give the answer in the tutorial group.
C | 1 2 3 4 5 | I prepare the contents carefully for myself before the reporting phase.
D | 1 2 3 4 5 | In this group, we are easily satisfied with a particular solution or explanation.
E | 1 2 3 4 5 | I think the other groups have already done more than we have.
F | 1 2 3 4 5 | I learn a lot from the contributions of other group members.
G | 1 2 3 4 5 | This is a productive tutorial group.
H | 1 2 3 4 5 | Responsibility for the content progress of this group is carried by all its members.

2
How do we work on the problems?

A | 1 2 3 4 5 | We work with a distinct agenda in this group.
B | 1 2 3 4 5 | Points on the agenda are actually dealt with in this group.
C | 1 2 3 4 5 | Everyone in this groups sticks to what was agreed.
D | 1 2 3 4 5 | Analysing a new problem is done too superficially.
E | 1 2 3 4 5 | Learning objectives are formulated explicitly in this group.
F | 1 2 3 4 5 | The synthesis phase of learning objectives adds little to what I already know.
G | 1 2 3 4 5 | We digress a lot in this group.
H | 1 2 3 4 5 | Decision-making works well in this group.

3

How effective is the teamwork?

A 1 2 3 4 5 We really listen to each other in this group.
B 1 2 3 4 5 I feel I can express my views in this group.
C 1 2 3 4 5 We trust each other's contributions in this group.
D 1 2 3 4 5 The views of certain group members are accepted too easily.
E 1 2 3 4 5 I am motivated and encouraged by other members in the group.
F 1 2 3 4 5 I feel at home in this group.
G 1 2 3 4 5 People in this group are open to different points of view.
H 1 2 3 4 5 People in this group are prepared to resolve differences of opinion.

4

The teaching materials

A 1 2 3 4 5 The module is clearly structured.
B 1 2 3 4 5 The problems require lots of discussion.
C 1 2 3 4 5 The module offers enough opportunities for revision and application.
D 1 2 3 4 5 The module has a varied content.
E 1 2 3 4 5 The problems present me with sufficient opportunity to develop my own initiatives.
F 1 2 3 4 5 So far, the problems have challenged me to carry out further analysis and studying.
G 1 2 3 4 5 The set-up of the module makes me feel that I am gaining insight into subjects relevant to this course.
H 1 2 3 4 5 Books and other learning tools enable me to do useful work on the learning objectives.

5

The discussion leader

A 1 2 3 4 5 The discussion leader stuck to the agenda.
B 1 2 3 4 5 The discussion leader encouraged the group to make clear choices when dealing with the problems.
C 1 2 3 4 5 The discussion leader frequently summarised the discussion.
D 1 2 3 4 5 The discussion leader prevented us from deviating from the topic.
E 1 2 3 4 5 The discussion leader dominated the discussion.
F 1 2 3 4 5 The discussion leader paid too little attention to individual contributions.
G 1 2 3 4 5 The discussion leader made sure that the group tackled the problems according to the agreed procedure.
H 1 2 3 4 5 The discussion leader made sure that the group formulated clear learning goals.

6
The tutor

A [1|2|3|4|5] The tutor stimulated progress in the group from a content point of view.

B [1|2|3|4|5] The tutor helped us to see the links between different parts of the course content.

C [1|2|3|4|5] The tutor was able to give a good description of collaboration within the group.

D [1|2|3|4|5] The tutor directed the way we think about the subjects in the course

E [1|2|3|4|5] The tutor left too much to us.

F [1|2|3|4|5] The tutor explained so much to us that I ended up doing less study on my own.

G [1|2|3|4|5] The tutor offered different alternatives, from which we could make a choice.

H [1|2|3|4|5] The tutor thought with us starting from our prior knowledge of the topic.

7
Summarising

A [1|2|3|4|5] The summaries were short.

B [1|2|3|4|5] The summaries reflected the different opinions in the tutorial group.

C [1|2|3|4|5] The summaries were accurate.

D [1|2|3|4|5] The timing of the summaries was well chosen.

E [1|2|3|4|5] The summaries guided the discussion.

F [1|2|3|4|5] The summaries were supported by visual aids.

G [1|2|3|4|5] The meeting would have been more productive if summaries had been given more frequently.

H [1|2|3|4|5] After the summary, the group was given the opportunity to comment on it.

3 Checklist: 'Skills of a tutorial group member'

Below is a checklist presenting the most important collaborative activities a tutorial group member can offer in tutorial group meetings.
- Study this checklist carefully. Think about your own behavior as a group member.
- Score your behavior by indicating whether you perform certain skills often, sometimes or never.
- Then ask fellow group members if they have also observed the presence or (partial) absence of specific skills. Ask your peers for feedback.
- Note the (sub)skills you want to improve and check regularly whether you have succeeded.

Checklist: 'Skills of a tutorial group member'

Skill	Characteristics	Often	Sometimes	Never
Listening in an active way Understanding the messages of others	• Regular eye contact • Listening to the whole story before reacting • Few interruptions • Noting the essence of the message • Avoiding personal interpretations • Checking if the other understands • Showing interest by non-verbal signals			
Giving information Actively telling your fellow students about your ideas, completing information from others, clarifying obscurities	• Organising your thoughts in advance • Distinguishing between main and secondary points • Expressing thoughts clearly • Talking in a lively manner • Distinguishing between objective facts and personal opinions • Avoiding information overload (too much at once)			
Asking for information Requesting clarification or further information	• Formulate questions brief and clearly • Formulate unambiguous questions • Questions are on topic • Asking open questions properly • Asking closed questions properly			
Making summaries Arranging (parts of) the discussion	• Making clear that you want to summarise • Conveying the main ideas of the discussion • Offering an accurate representation of the discussion • Presenting the summary at the right time			

Skill	Characteristics	Often	Sometimes	Never
Evaluation Appraising the quality of group progress with regard to content, procedures and interactions	• Observing processes in a purposeful and systematic way • Being able to treat events and incidents in concrete terms • Being able to express either positive or negative opinions • Being able to offer suggestions for improvement • Being able to stick to agreements for change			
Giving feedback Offering reactions to the behavior of group members	• Being constructive • Commenting on specific behavior • Being concrete • Considering feelings (being tactful) • Presenting the feedback in the 'I'-form • Offering feedback relevant to the group • Offering practical solutions/alternatives for specific behavior • Aware of how feedback is received			
Receiving feedback Being able to evoke responses on the effect your behaviour has on group members	• Listening openly and undefensively • Asking for more information when the feedback is vague • Verifying whether your own interpretation of the feedback is correct • Working out for oneself whether your behaviour has the desired impact • Thinking about the way you can change/improve your behavior			
The scribe Being able to organise data and apply visual aids describing the exchange of information	• Being able to derive important information from the discussion • Being able to present information in keywords, abbreviations or symbols • Being able to develop schemas, concept maps, diagrams • Being able to distinguish objective information from personal opinions			

6 Chairing a tutorial group meeting

6.1 Introduction

The role of the discussion leader was briefly introduced in Chapter 3. Tutorial sessions need to be structured well in order to be effective. Good working procedures, a good working climate and good management of the discussion are all important. The discussion leader has a special responsibility in achieving these. Chairing a meeting is something which most students will be unfamiliar with at the beginning of their studies. For this reason, the next few section focus on the important aspects of the discussion leader's role. Choosing the chair is discussed in the following section. Then some general points about the role of the discussion leader are raised in section 6.3. The task-oriented aspects are discussed in sections 6.4 and 6.5. The group-related functions are dealt with in paragraph 6.6. The chapter finishes with some final observations.

6.2 Taking turns

In a tutorial, the role of discussion leader is usually rotated so that each member of the group takes it on at least once per course. During the first meeting, group members should decide who will be discussion leader at which meeting. The list of names of group members can serve as a basis for the sequence in which you undertake this task. When group members know when their turn will be well in advance, then you can make adequate preparations. If a discussion leader is randomly appointed at the start of a meeting, it increases the chances of the job being done inadequately.

There are two suitable moments to rotate the role of discussion leader. The first is to change the leader for each new meeting. The allocated person then leads the meeting for the whole two hours, thus chairing both the synthesis phase of one problem as well as the analysis phase of the new problem. When the discussion leader has functioned as scribe in the preceding meeting, he or she will be well prepared to undertake the role of discussion leader in the next meeting.
The second way is to switch roles during a meeting. This procedure works as follows: group member A is discussion leader from the start of a new problem up to and including the synthesis of that problem at the next meeting. Group member B takes over when the next new problem is discussed and also chairs the reporting phase in the next meeting. This means that both analysis and synthesis phases of a problem are in the same hands. This method has considerable advantages for discussion leaders as they can prepare for the synthesis phase in between meetings at home.
You will need to choose between these two options at the start of each course unit.

6.3 Some general points

Effective discussion leaders can make an important contribution to the progress made by the group as far as content and process are concerned. By preparing well, by being alert to the activities occurring while discussing the problem, by a certain amount of methodological persistence, and by intervening in time when members lapse into dysfunctional behaviour the discussion leader can make a positive contribution to both task-related and group-related processes during tutorial group meetings.

Before examining the various tasks of the discussion leader in more detail, we would like to clear up a common misunderstanding. Many students believe that the discussion leader holds a pivotal position with regard to the success or failure of the tutorial. They tend to look upon the discussion leader as the sole person responsible for overall group functioning. If the tutorial goes off the rails, accusing fingers are all too often pointed at the discussion leader, e.g. for failing to make a timely intervention, neglecting to outline the main points or pursue a particular line of questioning. Clearly the discussion leader does hold a significant position in stimulating and monitoring the progress of the tutorial meeting, but we believe that all group members are responsible for making their own contributions, thus ensuring the progress of the discussion as a group. This mean you can't just put your feet up and relax when it's someone else's turn to be discussion leader. If the tutorial gets bogged down or important aspects of the discussion are omitted, it is the job of every group member to point this out and act upon it.

You might ask yourself why a discussion leader is necessary at all if everyone in the group takes joint responsibility for its progress. Indeed, if all group members were capable of focusing their attention on the content of the discussion at the same time as ensuring its continuity, a discussion leader would not be needed. Experience has shown, however, that functioning as a group member and steering the discussion is a combination very difficult to achieve. Members of a tutorial group are often so involved in the issues under discussion that they are unreceptive to the contributions of others or unaware of the direction in which the discussion is going. This is why we need to have someone less involved in the issues being explored. This person must be able to maintain an objective overview and intervene when co-operation breaks down. A discussion leader is expected not only to monitor the rate of progress of the learning process, but also the way in which group members interact during the discussions. A good discussion leader is particularly interested in the way in which the group works on a problem. Therefore, discussion leaders should preferably not get too involved in discussing the actual content of the problem. Experience shows that, alas, they do this too often, they won't achieve much of their own special responsibilities.

A tutorial meeting usually consists of two main activities: exploring a new problem (analysis phase) and integrating the material studied in relation to the learning objectives set at the previous tutorial (synthesis phase). As most tutorial groups start off their meetings with a synthesis phase, we will deal first with preparation a discussion leader needs for this part of the meeting. Subsequently, we will discuss the preparation required for the analysis phase.

6.4   The role of the discussion leader during the synthesis phase

The discussion leader can best prepare for the synthesis phase by thoroughly studying the learning objectives of the previous session. Once you have done this, you might consider the following aspects prior to the tutorial.
- Is there a particular relationship between the learning objectives?
- Will you need to discuss the learning objectives in a particular order?
- How much time will you likely need for discussing the learning objectives? How much time should be devoted to each of these?
- What difficulties are there in the subject matter to be studied? When and how will you pay attention to these?
- What could be the connecting link between the theme of the module, the problems and the learning objectives stemming from these? Can you derive any general rules, principles or opinions from the material to be studied which go beyond the bounds of the specific learning objectives?
- What can you expect from the other members of the group based on their performance at other meetings and during the problem analysis phase of the previous meeting?
- Do you anticipate any difficulties arising from the way some group members acted in previous meetings? Do you have any ideas on how to tackle inadequate behaviour if it comes up again?

As we've mentioned already on several occasions throughout this book, a great deal of work needs to be done during the two hours spent in a tutorial. Therefore it is useful for the discussion leader to draw up an *agenda* at the start of the meeting. This agenda indicates how much time is available for each of the learning objectives and the analysis of the new problem. The agenda should make clear which issues will be discussed in which order and the time available. The discussion leader should break the agenda down into the number of items and allocate the time necessary for dealing with each topic.

The aim of the synthesis phase is to find out whether the members of the tutorial group now have a deeper understanding of the information studied. In-depth understanding means that you have recognised the structure in the information. You are able to distinguish between the main and the secondary matters, see the connections between the various units of information and have a clear idea of the main principles, mechanisms or processes in the material studied. You have tried to translate abstract information into concrete proposals and have seen whether you can apply the new information to the original problem. Finally, you have thought critically about what you have studied.

The phase of synthesis must enable the students to find out whether their understanding of the new subject is accurate and complete. For this purpose the group must allow questions to be raised to clarify sections of the material studied that are not yet clearly understood and open up possibilities for discussing the implications of the subject in relation to related problems or future professional activities. The synthesis must not become simply a chain of unrelated and independent subjects but must be given a place within the framework of the theme or sub-theme of the course. Regular reference to the theme or sub-theme leads to a better structuring and integration of the subject matter.

At the begin of a tutorial meeting the discussion leader presents the agenda and finds out whether the other members of the group will go along with the order of the learning objectives and the amount of time allocated to them. The agenda is an aid to structure the discussion; it should allow for a certain flexibility. If the discussion of a particular subject takes longer than expected and the members of the group find prolongation of the discussion useful, the agenda must not become a straitjacket that prevents this. It should be possible to modify the order of the meeting. After the group members have agreed upon the agenda, the chair should ask group members to tell each other about the learning resources they have studied. Make a brief inventory of all the literature, audiovisual or electronic (Internet) sources that have been consulted in order to find information. Doing this allows group members to become aware of other interesting sources available; it offers insight into different aspects which may form another basis of discussion and it gives students an idea whether everyone has done what was agreed upon.

After this inventory of learning resources comes the first learning objective on the agenda. The discussion leader's introduction should not be left to a simple summing up of the learning objective and procedurally vague opening statements such as 'How does X happen?' or 'Who's found out something about this?'. Such statements give little direction and do not motivate. As a discussion leader, it is better to begin with a short summary of the discussion that led to the formulation of the learning objective in the last meeting, specifying the objective and indicating how it should be dealt with in the current tutorial.
A good approach to follow might go somewhat like this: 'Last time we discussed the ways in which X could occur. You held varying opinions. Some thought that X was a consequence of Y. Others put forward opposing arguments, Z, A and B. Let's first see what the different authors have to say on the topic and then go on to discuss any problems you encountered while studying the literature. Diana, last time you suggested that Y caused X. What do you think now after studying the literature?'
This kind of opening statement has the following characteristics: the discussion leader clearly places the problem in context, encourages fellow students to contribute and puts forward a plan for discussing the subject in question. By introducing the learning objective like this the discussion leader gets the meeting off to an active start and by addressing people by name the leader is stimulating group members to make their own contributions.

Having studied the material carefully, as discussion leader you will have plenty of information at your fingertips. Use this knowledge to structure the discussion and pose questions. But don't fall into the trap of contributing too actively in any discussions related to content for doing that won't help you do the leader's job properly. If the chair must contribute, be concise. During synthesis of the studied information, the chair should ensure that the flow of information is both manageable and kept focused. To achieve this, you have a number of options. First, allow those who wish to speak to do so. Simply saying the name of the person who wants to contribute helps keep the meeting in order and stops others from talking at the same time. A condition here, naturally, is that you are paying close attention and recognise the verbal or non-verbal signs that someone is getting ready to say something. Making regular eye contact with other members is important. Therefore, it's useful to arrange the seating in the room so that you can see all that is going on.

Secondly, remain alert for opportunities to increase the input of information. Discourage the students from talking too much about the facts. Invite group members to distinguish the main points from the secondary ones, ask for clarification if someone's explanation is not clear, stimulate the drawing of visual aids, diagrams and such on the board, invite students to add to examples and encourage them to examine interpretations, viewpoints or conclusions in a critical way (see box 26 in Chapter 3 for a summary of important learning activities). Meanwhile the chair should also guard against interactions taking place solely between himself or herself as discussion leader and an individual group member. You have to support the exchange of information among all group members.

Thirdly, it's important not to let the discussion go off-topic. Drifting gradually on to another subject thwarts the orderly discussion of a problem in any depth or with fruitful results. This may happen when participants don't entirely understand one another. Summarising the discussion is a good way of preventing drift: a summary confronts the group with its own progress and gives an opportunity to focus attention on the discussion goal. The chair can also add structure to the discussion by encouraging the scribe to make notes on the board, by rephrasing information that has been presented thus far and by drawing conclusions. The actual synthesis should not be a sequence of unrelated subjects, but must be placed in the context of the problem studied or the theme or sub-themes offered in the module. Referring regularly to those themes will help the group members to structure and integrate the study material for themselves.

Rounding off a discussion well helps students to organise new information. A good way of doing this is to review the main points of what has been learnt, e.g.: 'We've now taken an in-depth look at the issue and spent a considerable amount of time discussing U, V and W. Does anyone have anything to add? No? Then I'd like to recap on the main points. First X, then Y, and finally Z.' The discussion leader will be stimulating fellow group members during the closure to also review the points of the discussion and decide whether they have gained new knowledge and insights.

Box 33 gives an overview of the most important activities a discussion leader should carry out during the synthesis phase. Appendix 1 in this chapter presents a checklist which can be used in tutorial meetings to observe a group member in the role of a discussion leader during the synthesis phase.

Box 33 *Activities of a discussion leader during the phase of synthesis*

- Give the group members an agenda for dealing with the various learning objectives.
- Make an inventory of the sources studied.
- Open the discussion of the learning objectives in an adequate manner by referring back to the initial analysis and reminding fellow group members how the learning objectives were arrived at.
- Encourage the provision of information from the group members by:
  - inviting them to pick out what is relevant in the information they have found;
  - stimulating the break down the information into main and secondary points;
  - asking for clarification when an explanation is unclear;
  - encouraging members to ask each other questions and to give explanations;
  - asking for examples;
  - stimulating the drawing of connections between related parts of the subject matter;
  - asking for links to be made between the new material and the whole theme or sub-theme from the course book;
  - encouraging diagrams to be drawn and developed on the board;
  - summarising regularly or asking others to do so;
  - encouraging students to review the original problem critically in the light of the information studied.
- Encourage the members of the group to participate in the discussion.
- Suggest evaluations of the way in which:
  - the group is making progress with the subject matter;
  - students are studying or reporting;
  - students are work together and participating in discussion.

6.5 The role of the discussion leader during the analysis phase

The discussion leader also has an important role when dealing with a problem in the analysis phase. Prior to the tutorial you should consider a few points. You are not expected to actually crack the problem yourself before the session starts, but you should read up on it before. Take a good look at any advice the module designers gives on potential approaches to the problem. Sometimes you can find additional information in the module book or on the electronic work environment. All this may give you some basic ideas for helping the group decide how to tackle this problem.

The first thing to address in the tutorial session is the procedure the group will follow when working on the problem. Once a procedure has been agreed upon you must ensure the group sticks to it. If the group begins deviating, it is your job to point this out and to lead them back. Sometimes however, you will have to be open to adopting a new manner of working.

During problem analysis the discussion leader should be very aware of *increasing the input of information*. The aim is to have group members put forward hypotheses, theories, processes, mechanisms or procedures that offer explanations or solutions for understanding or solving the phenomena or events described in the problem. You can encourage this in all sorts of ways, e.g. by asking questions or by stimulating the group members to ask each other questions, by paying attention to divergent opinions, by responding to signals of non-verbal behavior, by summarising differences of opinion. Make sure that everyone gets enough opportunities to put forward their hypotheses or suggestions and that ideas are developed in-depth. During this phase it's important that the discussion leader also encourages the members of the group to bring in their prior knowledge. Help group members to associate information, create an environment where everybody feels safe and is open to each other. Start with the brainstorm technique and stick to the rule that bringing in ideas is strictly separate from working out the ideas or criticising them.

As discussion leader you must guard against placing too much emphasis on maintaining a smooth progress during the initial discussion. The aim of this phase is to reactivate knowledge that you already have and to develop theories and suggestions that can steer the self-directed learning process. Different insights, opposing suggestions and diverging conclusions are part of this and are, therefore, not a sign of little progress. The very differences in insights and opinions backed up by arguments actually make tutorial group meetings lively and exciting. Naturally, in this phase as well, you should also try to structure and channel information. Skills such as summarising, reformulating and structuring information are necessary to avoid rambling discussions. Prevent those by having the ideas expressed by the group worked out on the board in a schematic form. The discussion of new problems should result in the formulation of learning objectives. The analysis of a new problem is only a success if it lays down a foundation for the challenging self-study to be done in the following days.

Box 34 presents an overview of the most important activities that a discussion leader can carry out during the analysis phase. Appendix 2 offers an observation list which can be used in a tutorial meeting to observe a discussion leader chairing the group during the phase of analysis.

Box 34 *Activities of a discussion leader during the phase of analysis*

- Introduce a new problem in an adequate manner.
- Propose a procedure for discussing the problem.
- Make sure the agreed upon procedure is followed.
- Support the tutorial group in formulating the choice of problem definition.
- Increase the input of information from the group members during the initial discussion of the problem by:
  - stimulating brainstorming by promoting free associative thinking and discouraging premature criticism;
  - encouraging a wide variety of explanations and opinions;
  - allowing attention to be paid to alternative ideas, theories, suggestions or solutions; noting contrasting visions and stimulating the group members to discuss these in depth;
  - paying attention to schematic presentations of ideas on the board;
  - summarising regularly or inviting others to do so.
- Help to develop thorough and precise learning objectives and guide the decision process.
- Encourage all members of the group to participate.

6.6 Stimulating a collaborative working atmosphere

Besides the activities mentioned previously, the discussion leader must also pay attention to the *manner* in which group members take part in the discussion. A group that interacts well doesn't just come from nowhere. Each new group will have participants unsure of themselves to some extent or other. They'll be asking themselves questions like: 'Will the others accept me? Will my contribution be appreciated? Will a certain degree of openness and collective trust emerge in this group? Is this group capable of attaining the goals it has set itself? Will I feel comfortable in this group?' Group members bring all these uncertainties along when they start working together. In working together on shared goals, they will be trying to answer these questions. Finding answers and matching up the different expectations of each member are important elements in the *co-operative process*. It usually takes a couple of tutorials before the group finds its feet in terms of effective collaboration.

The discussion leader can be instrumental in creating the right conditions for the development of the group. Adopting a neutral stance in the discussion will make it is easier for him to focus on the way in which group members participate. From this slightly detached position, the discussion leader will be able to determine whether a particular individual feels at ease, whether contradictions that surface are constructively or personally intended, and whether all contributions receive sufficient attention. The discussion leader can also influence the collaborative climate of the tutorial, e.g. by involving group members in the discussion, by preventing certain individuals from being intimidated, and by stimulating an evaluation about the way in which the group co-operates. By encouraging participation in the discussion, by showing interest in other people's ideas, by reconciling differing standpoints, by making a joke at a suitable moment or allowing other group members to do so, the discussion leader is able to ensure that the other members of the tutorial group not only feel involved in the subject matter, but also experience the tutorial group as a collaborative platform for their studies that permits interaction to take place in an open and safe atmosphere (see box 27).

In Chapter 3, our attention focused on different behavioural patterns presenting in the tutorial group. These behavioural patterns affect the way in which the discussion acquires form and content. Some members like to talk a lot, others will prefer to sit back and listen to what's being said, whilst others will prefer to disagree with assertions made by others. The discussion leader will be confronted with these behavioural patterns but must make sure that the structure of the discussion remains intact. This is no easy task. Despite all the good intentions of group members to collaborate, they can make life very difficult for the discussion leader.

We shall now provide a few examples of the problems that might arise and the options available for overcoming these.

The student who barely contributes to the discussion
Some students make little effort to contribute towards the discussion. Of course, this does not necessarily reflect the amount of work that the student may have carried out beforehand. It might have something to do with the character and upbringing of the individual. The reasons why a person might prefer to stay silent are numerous. For instance, individuals might feel that (justifiably or otherwise) they have nothing to contribute to the discussion or get the impression that every time they want to say something someone else prevents them from doing so by interrupting. It might just be a reluctance to say anything as a reaction to an unfavourable experience at a previous tutorial.
Only a discussion leader capable of observing the way in which individuals take part in the discussion can effectively draw in the quieter members of the group. The discussion leader must be able to pick up the non-verbal signals, e.g. by stating: 'I see that you don't completely agree with what is being said, can you tell us what you think about it?' Sometimes it is useful to involve somebody spontaneously: 'Peter, what do you think about this?', or by indicating the value of somebody's contribution: 'Anne, that's an interesting perspective you brought forward!'

The long-winded student
Some tutorial group members like to get their ideas, experiences and interpretation of the study material across at any price. Their contributions become a mishmash of words and fail to make any impact. A long and laborious presentation might indicate that the individual is having some trouble in getting to

grips with the study material. Stopping the student outright may not be the best option for the discussion leader. Doing so may be seen as a criticism and could result in the student simply clamming up or making frantic efforts to explain everything all over again. If the presentation is too long-winded, the discussion leader should attempt to summarise it by emphasising the key elements contained within it. For example: 'Paul, if I understood you correctly, there are two points which you wish to make, firstly..., secondly.... Did I understand you correctly?' If the student continues to ramble on, the discussion leader will have no alternative but to intervene: 'Okay Paul, thank you, I think Lisa has something to say on the subject now.'

The student who keeps changing tack

Some students are inclined to digress into areas that may be related to the main subject matter, but which are not relevant in the context of the discussion. This kind of digression away from the original subject matter is one of the most common problems in a group discussion and inhibits progress to such an extent that other members of the group will also start to go off at a tangent. In these circumstances, the discussion leader would be wise not to respond to the content of the presentation. By giving students the opportunity to explain the relevance of their presentations, you will be allowing the discussion to wander further away from its original objective. Instead, the discussion leader should point out that the discussion was beginning to stray from the subject matter, reiterate the main issues and ask if anyone would like to add anything.

The free-rider

A well-known problem in groups and subgroups is the problem of free riders, members who try to benefit from the efforts of others without investing much of their own energy and time in group productivity. In the beginning it is quite hard to realise when members have these intentions. They seem co-operative, bring in opinions and agree with the arrangements the group has made. More and more frequently, however, they come up with excuses for not carrying out their own part of the work of the group. After a while other group members begin responding non-verbally to the excuses, showing their irritation at their peer's behaviour. Before tension in the group rises too high, the chair should lead the group in discussing their observations and feelings about the free rider. In an evaluation session the discussion leader should invite the members of the group to put forward their feedback. An important part of the feedback should be the effect the free-rider's behaviour has on their readiness to continue the collaboration, e.g., the irritation they feel which hinders their participation to the group in general, tactics they use to exclude the free rider from getting information, etc. The free rider will, of course, get an opportunity to respond. By the end of the feedback session the group members should have set clear agreements on how the (non)contributions of free-riders behavior will be dealt with in future. At appropriate moments the group should share their experiences of the new, improved cooperative working style of the (hopefully) ex-free rider. As handling free riders can generally be hard for students the tutor should support them in steering the group away from less co-operative group behaviour.

Box 35 offers an overview of some important activities that a discussion leader can do to stimulate collaboration in the tutorial group.

Box 35 *Activities of a discussion leader in stimulating collaboration between tutorial group members*

- Be open to the way group members participate in the discussion.
- Do not focus exclusively on the content.
- Pay attention to behaviour that promotes collaboration e.g. encouraging participation, being a door-opener, expressing group feelings and listening actively.
- When you observe behavior that causes hinderance at either the task or group level try, first of all, to avoid this behaviour indirectly. If you don't succeed, try the direct approach.
- Do not avoid evaluations during or at the end of a group meeting. Invite group members to analyse the way they collaborate and offer your observations and feelings by giving effective feedback.

6.7 Some final points

When you are first confronted with the task of being a discussion leader you will notice that it is not always easy to keep an eye on everything at the same time. The role is complex and requires you to multi-task several elements simultaneously. You may feel like a beginning juggler trying to keep a number of plates spinning on top of sticks all at the same time. If you are new to the role of discussion leader, try not to worry too much about whether the discussion is running smoothly. The aim of the tutorial group is to compare and contrast the information that has been acquired by each group members and to develop ideas that can help guide the study process in the right direction. Differences in interpretation, contrasting hypotheses and diverging conclusions are all part and parcel of this process and are by no means a sign that the tutorial is not progressing as it should. Try not to impede progress by sticking to a set way of working or thinking. Tutorials will thrive when well-argued differences of opinion are presented.

It's a good idea to talk with the tutorial group or the tutor about how you performed as a discussion leader. Feedback from others can be a useful source of information to improve your skills in this area. The reactions of others can provide useful information for improving your skills as a discussion leader. Appendix 3 of this chapter is a an observation scheme that you and your fellow group members can use to systematically observe the role of the discussion leader and collate information on what went well and what can be improved.

Particularly during the early stages of your studies, the tutor will act as personal coach to the discussion leader. Don't be afraid to ask the tutor's advice about your performance in this role and for practical suggestions on how you could improve your skills. The tutor will sometimes take the initiative to keep a discussion in progress by asking questions, offering suggestions for a new direction or by giving a summary. Some discussion leaders experience these interventions by the tutor as an implicit criticism of the way they are functioning, shut down and leave the rest of the discussion to the tutor. It is more sensible, however, to take note of the contributions the tutor makes and what you could learn from them. And if you really do become annoyed by the tutor's (too frequent) contributions, don't be afraid to ask to discuss this after the tutorial meeting and explain how you feel.

Finally in appendix 4 we present a questionnaire, the so-called PROFiT list, which enables you to assess your progression with respect to working in a tutorial group, either as a group member or as a discussion leader. It also includes a scheme to register your progress.

Appendix: Tools to improve your skills as a discussion leader

Introduction

In this appendix we offer material which can be used to improve the various skills a discussion leader should have that will enable the leader to enhance not only the learning of fellow students but also the efficiency and effectiveness of collaboration in the tutorial group as a whole. Acquiring these skills now, during your study, and becoming able to use them well at a high level of performance will lead on to great advantages and opportunities in your later professional life. Someone able to support task-based activities and maintain a well-functioning group is highly rewarded in professional organisations.

The material on offer includes both observation lists as well as checklists. Use these tools on a regular basis to evaluate your own progress as well as that of your colleagues in developing proficiency in the skills. Please use the guidelines on effective feedback (see near the end of section 5.8) when you want to give other members information about their performance in the tutorial group.

Appendix 1 gives you the opportunity to observe some essential chairing skills in the synthesis phase of a tutorial group meeting.

Appendix 2 gives you the opportunity to observe some essential chairing skills in the analysis phase of a tutorial group meeting.

Appendix 3 is a checklist. It allows you to assess your progress as a group member in participating in tutorial group meetings.

Appendix 4 is intended to help you further develop your ability to function in groups. Both questionnaire and the plan allow you to reflect on various skills required for functioning profitably in a tutorial group or (project) team. Use the questionnaire as the foundation for receiving profitable feedback from your peers and tutors after you have scored your own performance yourself.

1 Observation form 'Discussion leader functioning in the synthesis phase'

General comments (Briefly note the observations on which you want to give feedback.)

• What I found good in general about the discussion leader (DL):
• What I found less good in general about the DL:

Specific comments (Briefly note the observations on which you want to give feedback.)

• How did the DL introduce an agenda and keep the group to it?
• How did the DL make an inventory of the sources studied?
• How did the DL introduce the learning objectives and ideas from the initial discussion?
• How did the DL keep the group to the agreed problem discussion procedure?
• How did the DL enhance the provision of information?
• How did the DL define main and secondary matters and integrate what had been studied?
• How did the DL ensure that what had been learnt was applied to the original problem?
• How did the DL ensure that an evaluation of our learning experiences was carried out?

I observed the following skills (tick):

Summarising	
Asking for more in-depth information	
Structuring / channelling	
Supporting integration of the subject matter	
Encouraging application of the subject matter	
Stimulating a critical appreciation of the subject matter	
Facilitating the participation of the members of the group	
Other, namely	

2   Observation form 'Discussion leader functioning in the analysis phase'

General comments (Briefly note the observations on which you want to give feedback.)

• What I found good in general about the discussion leader (DL):
• What I found less good in general about the DL:

Specific comments (Briefly note the observations on which you want to give feedback.)

• How did the DL introduced the new problem?
• How did the DL keep the group to the procedure agreed for discussion of the task?
• How did the DL support the tutorial group in formulating the description of the problem?

- How did the DL stimulate the analysis of the problem?

- How did the DL increase the input of information from the members of the group?

- How did the DL stimulate the tutorial group to formulate workable learning objectives?

- How did the DL help all members of the group to participate?

I observed the following skills (tick):

Stimulating ideas	
Clustering ideas	
Asking for more in-depth information	
Summarising	
Asking for specification information	
Restating / restructuring information	
Stimulating participation	
Other, namely	

3 Checklist: Discussion leader skills

Skill	Characteristics	Often	Sometimes	Never
Preparing the meeting Considering how the meeting can be run effectively and efficiently	• Thinking about the sequence of the learning objectives • Considering potential difficulties in the learning resources • Trying to estimate the participation levels of group members • Thinking about how the participation of group members can be stimulated or curbed (if necessary) • Preparing for the new problem at hand • Considering the best procedure for analysing the new problem • Developing a list of topics on an agenda			
Stimulating a focused working environment Channel, arrange, reformulate information in a coherent system	• Presenting an agenda and a working procedure • Presenting the learning objectives in a motivating way • Distinguishing between main and secondary points • Encouraging summaries • Stimulating the posing of questions • Limiting distractions • Fostering the use of visual aids e.g. concept maps, schemes, diagrams			
Encouraging concrete information	• Asking for concrete examples • Stimulating students to reveal personal experiences related to the subject			
Stimulating open and respectful exchange of information Looking for connections between the various aspects of the subject matter	• Asking for similarities and differences • Comparing theories, models • Looking for the connection between the problem at hand and the (sub)theme mentioned in the module book • Stimulating students to think about relevant analogies or metaphors			

3 Checklist: Discussion leader skills (continued)

Skill	Characteristics	Often	Sometimes	Never
Stimulating the application of information	• Applying the new information to the original problem • Analysing an analogue (similar) problem			
Stimulating critical appraisal of information	• Observing contradictory theories, models, arguments, ideas in the literature and between group members • Offering students the opportunity to present back-up arguments to defend contradictions • Exploring the strong and weak points of a theory, model or an argument			
Diagnosing how effectively the group is functioning	• Evaluating the quality of the meetings • Examining which learning activities are being omitted and finding ways to correct this • Exploring difficulties in knowledge exchange			
Stimulating participation by all group members	• Encouraging the quieter students to speak up • Keeping the more dominant students in check • Showing interest in others' ideas • Expressing appreciation for contributions			
Creating a harmonious and productive working environment	• Reconciling different viewpoints • Being open for jokes • Making tensions between group members a subject of discussion by observing them in time			

4   PROfessional Functioning in Teams (PROFiT)

Introduction

In the past a professional, such as a general practitioner, a lawyer, a medical specialist or an organisation consultant, usually worked alone in their own practice or independently within a large organisation. Nowadays, they work in health centres, partnerships or companies. The lonely professional doesn't exist any more; professionals are functioning more and more often in groups or teams both inside and outside organisations. The professional has definitely become an organisational creature. A large part of the professional's work takes place in all sorts of groups: departmental teams, self-directed teams, project groups, meetings and committees. As a student you must prepare yourself for this group work. Below you will find information about a fruitful way to do this.

Becoming aware of your own behaviour
In order to gain insight into how you are developing within the team you should reflect on the way you are working. Request feedback from your fellow students and tutors to gain valid information to base your reflections on. Feedback from others is more profitable when you have already thought carefully about how you function yourself. It becomes most useful when you first reflect on your own progress in a number of important aspects of professional functioning in teams.

The tool described below can be used to help you think about how you actually function in a team or group. The questionnaire is called 'PROfessional Functioning in Teams' (PROFiT). As you continue your studies you will get to know more about functioning in a team. Completing the questionnaire regularly will help you to identify your strengths and weaknesses. It will support your efforts in practising your new skills and provide you with help in asking for specific feedback from other members of the group. So, fill in this questionnaire on a regular basis, e.g., at the end of each course during the first year of study and at greater intervals later on.

The questionnaire is simple to complete. Just ask yourself whether you carry out a particular activity 'always', 'often', 'sometimes', 'seldom' or 'never' (the first column in the questionnaire) and take care to enter the appropriate score clearly. Perhaps at one stage or another you may not be able to answer all the facets of the questionnaire, e.g. because you haven't actually been a discussion leader yet. This is why we have added the 'Not applicable' category for your use, if necessary.

Use this questionnaire to reflect on the way in which you work in a team such as the tutorial group. This reflection process can be carried out using the following steps:

- Complete the first column of the questionnaire (My score). When doing so think about those activities that went well while you were working in your tutorial group. There is often a tendency to belittle skills that went well. This is not correct! Try also to give explicit attention to your strong points. Maybe you can develop these strong points even further or perhaps they can help you to compensate for your less strong side. There is nothing wrong with recognising that you can carry out certain activities well. Think also about the activities that didn't go down as well and could be improved. These must be points that you definitely want to tackle differently or better in the future.

- The next step is to check with fellow students and your tutor if they have experienced your observations in the same way. In other words, ask others for feedback about your strong and your less strong points. Try to find out in an open discussion how you behave in the tutorial group. In order to gain this insight it is handy to start off approaching the people you trust and feel safe with. When you have become more experienced in asking for and receiving feedback you should broaden the circle of people from whom you wish to receive feedback. If you don't do this then you run the risk of only receiving socially desirable answers that do not contribute anything real to improving your skills. Ask a fellow student to complete the second column of the questionnaire (Score by other student). Discuss any of their scores that differ more than 1 point from your own. Ask what they think of your functioning and how you could improve your skills. Do the same with your tutor (Score by tutor). Ask their opinion of your functioning in the tutorial group.

- Once you have gained better insight into your behaviour in the group the last step in the reflection process is to draft one or more learning objectives. These learning objectives must be as specific as possible. They can be derived from your own experiences in the tutorial group and from the feedback that you have received from the other members and from your tutor. Formulate learning objectives positively: what skills in the field of functioning in a team do you want to improve in the near future? An example is given here.
  - You believe that you are not very good at structuring the subject matter during the phase of synthesis. You have particular difficulty with summarising the discussion into the main points and secondary ones. You also note that you have difficulty in noticing in time that you are going off the point during a discussion and in stopping yourself from this. In forthcoming tutorial group meetings you will try more often to summarise parts of the discussion and to round off the discussion with an overview of what you believe the main points to be. You will restrict yourself from going off the point by continuously asking yourself whether the contributions being made by other members of the group are actually in line with the topic under discussion. You formulate the following learning objectives.
    - To be able to better structure the discussion in the tutorial group by summarising more regularly.

- To channel the discussion better by making sure that group members do not deviate from the central subject.
– Next you write down how you will actually achieve these learning objectives. For example:
  - I will try to do this by giving a summary regularly (at least 5 times).
  - I will ask myself regularly whether we are still on the right track. I will check this regularly (at least 5 times) with the other members of the group. When I notice that we are going off the point I will make a comment about this and try to get the group back to the original subject.

Below you find a plan that you can use to determine your learning objectives. Use this plan for every learning objective that you want to describe.

How skills are going at present:

. . . .

. . . .

. . . .

Comments from third parties: fellow students or tutor:

. . . .

. . . .

. . . .

My learning objective(s):

. . . .

. . . .

. . . .

Specific activities I will carry out in order to achieve these learning objective(s):

. . . .

. . . .

. . . .

The 'PROfessional Functioning in Teams' (PROFiT) questionnaire

Score: 1 = never; 2 = seldom; 3 = sometimes; 4 = often; 5 = always; 0 = not applicable

Item		My score	Student score	Tutor score
1.	I prepare thoroughly for tutorial group meetings.	1 2 3 4 5 0	1 2 3 4 5 0	1 2 3 4 5 0
2.	I am on time (also after breaks).	1 2 3 4 5 0	1 2 3 4 5 0	1 2 3 4 5 0
3.	I listen actively to contributions from others.	1 2 3 4 5 0	1 2 3 4 5 0	1 2 3 4 5 0
4.	I take an active part in the phase of analysis.	1 2 3 4 5 0	1 2 3 4 5 0	1 2 3 4 5 0
5.	I take an active part in the phase of synthesis.	1 2 3 4 5 0	1 2 3 4 5 0	1 2 3 4 5 0
6.	The content of my contributions is of high quality.	1 2 3 4 5 0	1 2 3 4 5 0	1 2 3 4 5 0
7.	I examine relevant literature as indicated by the course requirements.	1 2 3 4 5 0	1 2 3 4 5 0	1 2 3 4 5 0
8.	I am capable of clearly explaining in my own words the literature I have read.	1 2 3 4 5 0	1 2 3 4 5 0	1 2 3 4 5 0
9.	I examine extra relevant literature above and beyond the minimal requirements of literature sources.	1 2 3 4 5 0	1 2 3 4 5 0	1 2 3 4 5 0
10.	I make proposals in the tutorial group that can lead to a better discussion of the content.	1 2 3 4 5 0	1 2 3 4 5 0	1 2 3 4 5 0
11.	I suggest ideas that can improve cooperation.	1 2 3 4 5 0	1 2 3 4 5 0	1 2 3 4 5 0
12.	I create depth in the phase of synthesis by asking critical questions.	1 2 3 4 5 0	1 2 3 4 5 0	1 2 3 4 5 0
13.	I use techniques (such as concept mapping) to visualise the information clearly when possible.	1 2 3 4 5 0	1 2 3 4 5 0	1 2 3 4 5 0
14.	I am able to identify and explain differences and similarities between different approaches (models/ theories) of an issue in the literature.	1 2 3 4 5 0	1 2 3 4 5 0	1 2 3 4 5 0
15.	I am able to systematically appraise the weak and strong points of theories/models.	1 2 3 4 5 0	1 2 3 4 5 0	1 2 3 4 5 0
16.	I have an interested, open-minded attitude towards the group.	1 2 3 4 5 0	1 2 3 4 5 0	1 2 3 4 5 0
17.	I give feedback to other members of the group in an adequate manner.	1 2 3 4 5 0	1 2 3 4 5 0	1 2 3 4 5 0
18.	I am open to feedback from other group members.	1 2 3 4 5 0	1 2 3 4 5 0	1 2 3 4 5 0
19.	I carefully prepare my role as discussion leader.	1 2 3 4 5 0	1 2 3 4 5 0	1 2 3 4 5 0
20.	As discussion leader I enable other members of the group to participate.	1 2 3 4 5 0	1 2 3 4 5 0	1 2 3 4 5 0
21.	As discussion leader I structure the discussion in a fruitful way.	1 2 3 4 5 0	1 2 3 4 5 0	1 2 3 4 5 0
22.	As discussion leader I ensure that the discussion does not drift off the point.	1 2 3 4 5 0	1 2 3 4 5 0	1 2 3 4 5 0
23.	As discussion leader I stimulate group members to bring in divers ideas/ theories/solutions.	1 2 3 4 5 0	1 2 3 4 5 0	1 2 3 4 5 0
24.	As scribe I can summarise the various contributions of the group members coherently.	1 2 3 4 5 0	1 2 3 4 5 0	1 2 3 4 5 0

Write your general and specific observations at a separate sheet of paper.

Recommended literature

Adams, K., & Galanes, G.J. (2006). *Communicating in Groups. Applications and Skills*. Boston: McGraw Hill. (6th edition).

Barkley, E.F., Cross, K.P. Major, C.H. (2005). *Collaborative learning techniques*. San Francisco (CA): Jossey Bass.

Buzan, T. (2003). *The mind map book*. London: BBC. (4th edition).

Jaques, D. (2000). *Learning in groups. A handbook for improving group work*. London: Kogan Page (3rd edition).

Payne, E., & Whittaker, L. (2000). *Developing Essential Study Skills*. Harlow: Pearson Education.

Savin-Baden, M., & Wilkie, K. (Eds.) (2006). *Problem-based Learning Online*. Berkshire (UK): Open University Press.

Schmidt, H.G., & Moust, J. H. C. (2000). Processes that shape small-group tutorial learning: A Review of Research. In C.E.H.D.H. Evensen (Ed.), *Problem-based learning: A research perspective on learning interactions* (pp. 19-52). Mahwah, NJ: Lawrence Erlbaum.

Wong, L. (2006). *Essential Study Skills*. Boston: Houghton Mifflin Company (5th edition).

References

Bales, R.F. (1970). *Personality and interpersonal behaviour.* New York: McGraw Hill.

Benne, K., & Sheats, P. (1948). Functional roles of group members. *The Journal of Social Issues, 4 (2),* 41-49.

Grave, de W. S., Schmidt, H.G., & Boshuizen, H. P. A. (2001). Effects of problem-based discussion on studying a subsequent text: A randomized trial among first year medical students. *Instructional Science, 29* (1), 33-44.

Haugeland, J. (1985). Artificial intelligence: The very idea. Cambridge, MA: The MIT Press.

Keuzegids Hoger Onderwijs 2006-2007: Verzamelgids (Consumer Report Higher Education 2006-2007). (2006).). Leiden, the Netherlands: Hoger Onderwijs Persbureau.

Kiessling, C., Schubert, B., Scheffner, D., & Burger, W. (2004). First year medical students' perceptions of stress and support: a comparison between reformed and traditional track curricula. *Medical Education, 38* (5), 504-509.

Kuhnigk, O., & Schauenburg, H. (1999). Psychological wellbeing, locus of control and personality traits in medical students of a traditional and an alternative curriculum. *Psychotherapie Psychosomatik Medizinische Psychologie, 49* (1), 29-36.

Schmidt, H. G., & Moust, J.H.C. (2000). Processes that shape small-group tutorial learning: A Review of Research. In C.E.H.D.H. Evensen (Ed.), *Problem-based learning: A research perspective on learning interactions* (pp. 19-52). Mahwah, NJ: Lawrence Erlbaum.

Schmidt, H.G., Vermeulen, L., & Van der Molen, H.T. (2006). Longterm effects of problem-based learning: a comparison of competencies acquired by graduates of a problem-based and a conventional medical school. *Medical Education, 40* (6), 562-567.

Schuwirth, L.W., Verhoeven, B. H., Scherpbier, A.J., Mom, E.M., Cohen-Schotanus, J., Van Rossum, H. J. (1999). An inter- and intra-university comparison with short case-based testing. *Advances in Health Sciences Education: Theory and Practice, 4* (3), 233-244.

Vermunt, J. D. (1992). *Leerstijlen en sturen van leerprocessen in het hoger onderwijs - Naar procesgerichte instructie in zelfstandig denken* [Learning styles and regulation of learning in higher education -Towards process-oriented instruction in autonomous thinking] PhD thesis. Amsterdam/Lisse: Swets & Zeitlinger.

Vleuten, van der C.P.M., Schuwirth, L. W. T., Muijtens, A.M.M., Thoben, A.J.N.M., Cohen-Schotanus, J., & Van Boven, C.P.A. (2004). Cross institutional collaboration in assessment: a case on progress testing. *Medical Teacher, 26* (8), 719-725.

Index